Artist at Work, Proximity of Art and Capitalism

Artist at Work, Proximity of Art and Capitalism

Bojana Kunst

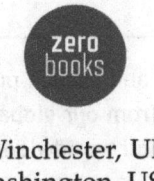

Winchester, UK
Washington, USA

First published by Zero Books, 2015
Zero Books is an imprint of John Hunt Publishing Ltd., Laurel House, Station Approach,
Alresford, Hants, SO24 9JH, UK
office1@jhpbooks.net
www.johnhuntpublishing.com
www.zero-books.net

For distributor details and how to order please visit the 'Ordering' section on our website.

Text copyright: Bojana Kunst 2014

ISBN: 978 1 78535 000 9
Library of Congress Control Number: 2015932361

All rights reserved. Except for brief quotations in critical articles or reviews, no part of this book may be reproduced in any manner without prior written permission from the publishers.

The rights of Bojana Kunst as author have been asserted in accordance with the Copyright, Designs and Patents Act 1988.

A CIP catalogue record for this book is available from the British Library.

Design: Stuart Davies

We operate a distinctive and ethical publishing philosophy in all areas of our business, from our global network of authors to production and worldwide distribution.

CONTENTS

Preface

Chapter 1: The Uneasiness of Active Art

Chapter 2: The Production of Subjectivity
2.1. The Crisis of Subjectivity
2.2. Problems with Profanation
2.3. The Work of the Performance Artist

Chapter 3: The Production of Sociality
3.1. The Glut of Sociality
3.2. Relational Delusions
3.3. The Working Spectator
3.4. Between One and Many: Collaboration
3.5. A Portrayal of Non-Functioning Community

Chapter 4: Movement, Duration and Post-Fordism
4.1. The Free Time of Dance
4.2. Slowing down Movement

Chapter 5: The Visibility of Work
5.1. The Artist as a Virtuoso
5.2. The Female Artist between Work and Life
5.3. The Artist's Time: Projective Temporality

Conclusion: On Laziness and less Work

Footnotes

Bibliography

"Work is Disease – Karl Marx."
Mladen Stilinović, 1981

Preface

The gestation of this book over the past few years is closely linked to my practical and theoretical work, which has, through lectures, workshops, dramaturgical work, work with producers and artists, travels, festivals and artistic residencies put me face to face with the recurrent questions of artistic powerlessness in relation to politics and contemporary methods of production. In experiencing this powerlessness, an interesting antagonism was always at work; personally, it disturbed me greatly and posed a number of questions for me, which in turn generated many reflections in this book. This antagonism can be briefly described as a contradiction between the forceful desire to create political and critical art, and the meek, almost 'martyr-like' recognition of the total appropriation of art by capitalism; any stance, no matter how critical and political, can easily find itself as just another in the offer of what Guillermo Gómez-Peña describes as *'mainstream bizarre'*. Of course, this forceful desire for political art, or the close link between creating art and political emancipation, has a long history in the art of the twentieth century. And yet, never before now has it been so widespread – today, it has actually become a lifestyle, particularly of those who don't have much to do with art, but crave the artistic style of living for this very reason. Art is thus in an interesting relationship with the functioning of contemporary capitalism which saturates all pores of social life: the criticism and the provocativeness of art seem to be a part of the exploitation of human powers.

A number of the texts that make up this book were written in a persistent search to understand art's political ambition and take it extremely seriously, affirm it through writing and thus also reflect on what is the relation between artistic work and artistic labour. I'm interested in analysing procedures and processes of contemporary art and using them to draw attention to the ambivalent proximity of art and capitalism, and through this critical proximity re-affirm art. And it is here that my reflections intertwine with what art produces in the proximity of capitalism; these questions must necessarily be tied to the methods of artistic work and production and in fact disclose what kind of worker an artist is, and what are then the forms of his (workers') revolt.

For this reason, I've divided my reflections in the book into several thematic clusters; they focus on fundamental human forces and powers; these are, today, in the centre of capitalist production, as well as in the centre of artistic interests. My approach to art is broad and inter-disciplinary: I often find a challenge and invitation to contemplation and argument formulation in artistic practices, but am less drawn to the analysis of individual works than I am to the thought that these works trigger, and their connection to philosophical questions about the characteristics of contemporary life. I focus particularly on those artistic practices of the last decades that can be broadly defined as performance or live arts – they range from performance art, contemporary dance and live events to contemporary theatre. Their research of new methods of work and performing show a clear political tendency.

In the first chapter titled 'About the Uneasiness of Active Art', I thus first write about the problems of political art and methods that tell us how to think the relationship between politics and art today. In the second chapter, 'Production of Subjectivity', I describe the role of performance and radical practices of art today, particularly in a time when one of the basic characteristics of contemporary work is becoming an unbroken transformation and performing of subjectivity. I want to show that it is precisely awareness about the conditions and methods of a performer's work (his work with subjectivity, self, body, etc.) that can bring these practices closer to an autonomous political and critical address. In the third chapter titled 'Production of Sociality' I tackle participatory art that focuses on social and community relationships, while at the same time I disclose certain processes of work in art, which have – in recent years – put cooperation and communities to the forefront. I wish to show through the labour of both artists and audiences, that it is possible to think the transformations of the public aspect of art, and show how such relationships should be placed in relation to the prevalence of communicative and linguistic labour today. In the fourth chapter 'On Movement, Duration and Post-Fordism' I use the case of contemporary dance to write about the central role of movement in capitalism, which is closely related to the progression of time and the establishment of new, flexible methods of work, and at the same time deeply effects articulation of new bodily practices. I'm interested in how it is possible – when we're thinking about movement as labour – to establish emancipation from flexibility and acceleration of life, and what is the role of art in all that. In the fifth chapter titled 'The Visibility of Work' I delve into the characteristics of the artist's work and mostly study how this work is a part of the production processes of contemporary capitalism (project work, precarious work, blurring the line between life and art). I study the qualities of artists' lives specifically because I'd like to draw attention to a different modality of artistic creation as useless spending and potentiality. In this chapter, I particularly follow critically, contemporary arguments that advocate the social role of art; through the artistic work I also rethink the argument about the economic effectiveness of art.

The main purpose of this book is the affirmation of artistic practice that happens through thinking about the economic and social conditions of the artist's work. Only then can it be revealed that what is a part of speculations of capital is not art itself, but mostly artistic life. It is the speculation about the ostensible freedom of artistic life that conceals the erasure of art from public space and increases the invisibility of its material and community processes. It turns out that prodigal and creative work of art today is extremely regulated, precisely because it is so close to, yet with its autonomy, so radically different from life.

In addition to new chapters, the book also contains a series of reworked essays I'd already published elsewhere. I wanted to retain the diffusion and variety of texts, and not deny conditions in which this theoretical work was mostly created: as a fruit of the very conditions of production and methods of work that I critically reflect upon. The conditions of precarious theoretical and research work result in topical writing, but this writing can be diffused and fragmentary, because it is difficult to keep its temporal continuity. At the same time, one can't naively believe in the illusory ability of uninterrupted transformation that is required by flexible work. And this is why, when I truly committed myself to writing this book, I found that my work, in different ways over the past few years, was marked by a couple of repeated and topical questions, and that through all the theoretical reflections a recognisable red thread is woven: an image of an artist at work.

The texts in the book are in large proportion a result of creative exchanges, particularly with other artists and writers throughout Europe, and also a result of numerous artistic and theoretical collaborations. During my travels, workshops, residencies and lectures I had a privilege to meet young artists and students in different artistic and academic environments and share with them acute and critical questions about the place of contemporary art, whilst making numerous friendships and collaborations that continue to this day.

I would like to thank the director of Maska Publishing Janez Janša and its editor Amelia Kraigher. The translator into English Urška Zajec worked meticoulously through the chapters in this book and gave them the final form in the English language. I also wish to thank many friends and colleagues for inspiring discussions: Ric Alshopp, Maaike Bleeker, Toni Cots, Bojana Cvejić, Danae Theodoridou, Begum Ercyas, Myriam van

Preface

Imschoot, Ivana Ivković, Bojan Jablanovec, Janez Janša, Janez Janša, Joe Kelleher, Gabriele Klein, Bara Kolenc, Andreja Kopač, Boyan Manchev, Tomislav Medak, Nana Miličinski, Aldo Milohnić, Bojana Mladenović, Ivana Müller, Nataša Petrešin Bachelez, Irena Pivka, Anja Planišček, Goran Sergej Pristaš, Vlado Gotvan Repnik, Martina Ruhsam, Alan Read, Paz Rojo, Danae Theodoriou, Hooman Sharifi, Ana Vujanović, Jasmina Založnik and Beti Žerovc. And I gracefully thank Igor for making love, not art.

Chapter 1

The Uneasiness of Active Art

> We could be easily frozen in this kind of pose, but no, we immediately begin to argue.
> (Builders, Chto delat 2005)

It is evident that the video by the British artist Carey Young takes place in one of the numerous offices of a modern high-rise corporation centre. The camera is focused on a woman in a dark blue business suit standing in front of a huge glass office wall. The woman keeps uttering a single sentence, using different accentuations, gestures and intonations in the process. She seems to be practising as though in a business presentation course. She pays attention to the pronunciation nuances and precise gesticulation while practising it over and over: "I'm the revolutionary."[1]

This unique exercise in style is a very good indication of the complex situation into which I want to place my reflection on the relationship between politics and contemporary art. We live at a time when creativity, a wish for change and constant reflection on creative conditions are the driving forces behind development in the post-industrial world, marked by the need to constantly revolutionize methods of production and creativity. Young's statement is therefore not only an exercise in style; this kind of 'coaching' is actually essential to the ways of working in contemporary capitalism, especially creative and artistic ways of working. In the contemporary corporate world, 'I'm the revolutionary' suddenly turns into a speech act *par excellence*. The transfer of the obsession with social change (which deeply marked the twentieth century) into a transparent sky-scraper helps us understand the topical social and political situation, which profoundly affects the way of thinking on the connection between politics and art, especially on the changed role of the autonomy of art today, which needs to be closely connected to artistic work itself. Today, politics is frequently understood as a system of organized interests, of bureaucratically structured activities planned in advance, and of organized and discursively conceptualized possibilities, which include various exercises in style in terms of artistic freedom. According to Slavoj Žižek, we now live in a world where pseudo-activity rather than passivity poses the basic threat. Furthermore, politics almost comes across as an urgency, as a coercion into constant participation and activity: "People intervene all the time, 'do something'; academics participate in meaningless debates and so on."[2] Žižek places this passivity in the opposition to the contemporary political situation, which, like many other theorists, he terms post-political, and one where we are faced with the reduction of politics to the expert management of social life.[3]

Arising from this post-political situation is a profound uneasiness that overcomes us when discussing the contemporary relationship between politics and art. At first sight, the art of today seems insufficiently engaged; artistic and creative powers seem more-or-less isolated from social contexts. It appears that today artistic freedom is proportionate to artistic unimportance or the powerlessness it exhibits as regards wider social change. The need for political art has never been at the foreground to the extent it is now; art has been called upon to comment on, document, discover and address political themes, as well as to actively intertwine with social and political participation processes.

Isn't this call for the politicization of art – the articulation of forums and conferences where politicization is discussed, of festivals that are being (sub)titled in this way, the differentiation between political and non-political generations – a sign of what Slavoj Žižek terms 'pseudo-activity'? Isn't the art of today deeply ingrained into the method of expertly managing social interests, a part of the contemporary urgency for ceaseless activity? Act, be active, participate, always be ready for opposition, generate new ideas, pay attention to contexts while constantly reflecting on your methods of production... Doesn't all that stand for the activity that profoundly defines the so-called post-political condition? In both visual art and the performing arts, political art is actually in good shape. It connects contexts, is topical, provokes, opens up forms of participation, is ceaselessly critical, reflexive, provocative and different. Art exists as the non-stop production of critical deviations and comments that are organised and intermediated through thematically oriented applications and pseudo-active models of the artistic market. Many contemporary art market contexts – exhibitions, productions and festivals – are based on a critical meta-language where art frequently appears as an autonomous field of freedom, different views and provocative creativity. Along with this meta-language, there is a growing political powerlessness of art, which seems increasingly isolated in its glass revolutionary tower. For this reason, Badiou finds that it is now constantly necessary to actively cover up the nothingness of what takes place, and makes the following statement at the conclusion of his manifesto of affirmationism: "It is better to do nothing than to contribute to the invention of formal ways of rendering visible that which Empire already recognises as existent."[4] The art of today seems to be generated in this field in-between pseudo-activity and the quest for a real effect; it is profoundly marked by the loss of the event and the desire for a radical cut at the same time.

The question I will therefore be discussing on many pages of this book is how artistic processes and creation intertwine with political processes, especially when they try to overcome positions of powerlessness and establish a new relationship with contemporary capitalist processes. I will show that, in order to critically understand this intertwinement of art and politics and also take a step forward from bemoaning the powerlessness of art, we need to rethink the relationship between art and ways of working. The ways in which the artist works today and the things produced by the artist's work place art intimately close to capitalism.

It is characteristic of the contemporary 'post-political' period that it no longer recognises the traditional twentieth century political artist, termed 'the party-member artist' by Oliver Marchart. This artist sacrifices part of their autonomy for the good of heteronomy – i.e. renounces the autonomy of art for the benefit of politics. As an illustration, Marchart offers the well-known dyptichon by Immendorf situated under the caption: *Where do You Stand with Your Art, Colleague? (Wo stehts du mit Deiner Kunst, Kollege?)* as a painter in his studio, with political demonstrations taking place outside his open door.[5] According to Marchart, the prevailing model of the political artist from the historical avant-gardes until the end of the 1960s was someone that constantly challenged the limits of autonomy in favour of politics, someone who constantly demolished the borders between art and other activities, between art and life. Today, this kind of activity seems naive if not anachronistic; contemporary artistic statements are articulated in the direction of the market, with the emancipatory power of creativity becoming the driving force of capital – whether we like it or not. As Marchart states, there is little we can do but ascribe ideological blindness to an artist who decides on autonomous heteronomy (because the party-member artist still believes in their own undiminished autonomy). In a world of politics as spectacle, creative economy and capital governed by institutionalized critical and political discourses, it is very hard to believe in the undiminished autonomy of the political artist who presents works at festivals of 'political art' and gives rise to provocative art at globalized festivals. Hence part of the disappointment in the artistic avant-garde and neo-avant-garde practices of the twentieth century, as their emancipatory power of liberating art and life goes well with the liberation power of capital: nowadays, creativity and artistic subjectivity are at the centre of the contemporary production of value.

The contemporary marketing of freedom and the transfer of revolutionary themes from the class struggle to the hedonistic entertainment industry and the creative industry of ideas has resulted in today's art rarely being articulated along the lines of revolutionary utopias and the emancipatory thinking of the future. If this does take place, it is usually in the form of specific pragmatically usable suggestions. For this reason, art frequently focuses on the production of the social; it is becoming a field and place of social relations, which is discussed in more detail in Chapter 3 of this book. Art frequently articulates its relationship with politics by inventing models of sociality and community, by active participation and interaction, and by means of propositions of and ways of meeting that constantly give rise to proposals for various forms of activities. This testifies to a problematic relation between art and the community; at the same time, this kind of politicization is close to another important artistic position that appears chiefly at the end of the twentieth century, replacing so-called party-member art.

According to Marchart, we now frequently face "heteronomous autonomy"[6] rather than autonomous heteronomy. Today, this is the prevailing hegemonic model of art. It is no longer about the party-member artist torn between loyalty to art on the one hand and the party on the other. As Marchart states, artists now adopt a position of pseudo-autonomy; they are subjectivised as creative joint-stock personalities or functioning service monads. The artist is their own (autonomous) entrepreneur and heteronomous (employee) at the same time. Interestingly enough, "at the moment of their greatest heteronomy (market dependence), these market entities harbour an auto-imagination of full autonomy."[7] If the politicization of art actually occurs, this is more or less to appease one's conscience, to draw from the joint pile of existing references that are to be discarded and replaced by a more effective offer at the first available opportunity. Although this kind of activity appears less anachronistic and more in accordance with the current social and political shifts, the basic political articulation of themes and contexts is still dictated by the market. The political stance of artists is similar to that of contemporary creative industries. They articulate their ideas by forming contexts and communicative social situations in advance, where particular relations can take place safely and without antagonism; this is where temporary communities can be formed, enabling the participation of different users, as well as the contingent and free-flow of various interests. It therefore seems as though it is actually the prevailing heteronomy that Žižek terms 'pseudo-activity'.

None of the two prevailing forms of twentieth century politicization give rise to political antagonism nowadays. Autonomous heteronomy is no longer the kind of politicization that can respond antagonistically to contemporary political reality. The party-member artist no longer has a field of activity; we could say they actually exist without a party. The actions of this kind of artist do not establish a potential for different political communities and forms of co-existence; today, it is no longer important which side artists sacrifice their autonomy for in terms of leaving art in order to set up a political community.

At the end of 2007, Slovenian theatre saw a very interesting attempt to re-topicalise the avant-garde political stance in *Ragged People/Pupils and Teachers (Raztrganci/Učenci in učitelji)*, a performance directed by Sebastijan Horvat. Not only did this engaged rendition of Matej Bor's agitation play take a direct stance on topical political events (especially toward the World War Two partisan movement in Slovenia and the current attempts to rehabilitate Nazi-sympathizing White Guard members), but also connected all this with the universal progressive values of resistance and radical affirmation, attempting to restore forgotten utopian twentieth century themes.

Director Sebastijan Horvat purposely staged *Ragged People* as an agitation for specific values, choosing its form along the same lines – an almost realistic agitation theatre performance that attempts to affirm the utopia of a more engaged world through a clear narrative about the incongruous oppositions of good and evil. However, there is a paradox in such autonomous heteronomy, where art makes a direct appeal yet addresses a group of people that has already been formed or 'subjectivised': a similar effect could be achieved if the political subject targeted by the performance was on the opposite side of the political spectrum. An agitation and production based on the other political perspective and foundations could have been equally successful. The politicization of art by abandoning artistic autonomy in order to establish progressive and engaged politics no longer has a direct effect in the post-political world because the artistic market offers various possibilities of political choice. The spectator communities established through these choices are not articulated through a political subjectivisation that is difficult and full of contradictions. Quite the opposite: the spectator communities are mainly articulated as pre-established moral communities that are formed along the dividing line between good and evil, where one's friends are suddenly separated from one's enemies. Today, the need for engaged theatre and art can frequently be discussed along the lines of what Chantal Mouffe terms "politics in the register of morality".[8] Her hypothesis is that, due to the disappearance of constitutive antagonism (which forms the essence of the political), political discourse is replaced by moral discourse. It is not that politics has been replaced by morality or that it has become more moral, but that it takes place though the register of morality. Political antagonisms are created as moral categories that contemporary communities identify with and thus become established in an imaginary way. It is no longer about the antagonism between those addressed by political articulations – between 'us and them' as bearers of certain articulations and forms of political subjectivisation. As Chantal Mouffe states, instead of a fight between the left and the right, we nowadays have a fight between those in the right and those in the wrong.[9] In this sense, the most radical works include those that do not allow us any possibility of choice, triggering uneasiness regardless of their political orientation – uneasiness at both the left and the right. This uneasiness is a consequence of the antagonism they create by means of their form (e.g. the Slovenian group Laibach), their anarchism (e.g. many anarchist works by Russian activists, such as Voina or some artistic predecessors at the beginning of the 1990s like Alexander Brenner or Oleg Kulik), or by means of a direct intervention into life itself (e.g. three Slovenian artists officially changing their name to Janez Janša, the name of former right wing Slovenian Prime Minister).

Therefore, art seems to be in a helpless position from the perspective of heteronymous autonomy as well, especially because artistic subjectivity is now at the centre of new models of creativity. Not only does art frequently function as an autonomous space of freedom, it also participates in a network of pre-established models of criticality and reflexivity, as a sort of 'politicisation with reason', or a choice between ready-made possibilities of discourse.

In contemporary performing arts, at least in the wider European space, it was held for a decade or so that the political was actually part of the form, of the way we make art, and thereby an answer to the question of what art is. From the middle of the 1990s onwards, through the practices of authors like Jérôme Bel, Xavier Le Roy, Janez Janša, Via Negativa, politicality was understood through an endless questioning and critique of the theatre apparatus itself and the relation to the audience. According to Bojana Cvejić, such questioning formed a kind of new regime of representation, which forms the tautological character of the performative. Here, the performance always questions and addresses the spectators in their role, leading them "to reflect upon their history, their taste, their capacity to perceive, the frames of references they should mobilize in order to be able to read the performance."[10] It is about the problematic status of post-modern theory, which becomes a sort of 'self-referential speech act', questioning the role of the spectator and revealing theatre in the role of the dispositive. This self-referentiality of one's own production conditions is at the centre of understanding contemporary post-political and pseudo-activity. Today, the facts that formed the basis of Benjamin's concept of political art at the beginning of the twentieth century have been radically changed.

In his famous essay *The Author as Producer* (1934), Benjamin rejects any kind of instrumentalisation of art for political purposes, stating that art is only political in the manner in which it observes the conditions of its own production; this means that it is aware of the production relationships within which it is generated and works towards emancipating these conditions. This emancipation of one's production conditions, the constant reflection on the models and protocols of production, is tightly connected to the contemporary models of production in the post-industrialised era. The creative solutions, the reflections on management hierarchies and non-material work forms of non-material work constantly place the author as producer into the very centre. From this perspective, we can even more accurately understand the 'powerlessness' of the artistic creator, constantly oscillating between various discursive models of specialized contexts shaped by curated contemporary festivals and many open methods of production that have seen market success.

Since contemporary politics renounces the constitutive dimension of the political, many philosophers see the political as within a deep caesura that, according to Chantal Mouffe, occurs as an ontic/ontological difference. She therefore proposes a differentiation between 'politics' and 'the political'; politics concerns daily political practices within which order is created, while the political concerns the manner of constituting society with antagonism as an essential characteristic.[11] The difference between politics and the police is also discussed by Rancière. According to him, the police is "organised as a set of procedures whereby the aggregation and consent of collectivities is achieved, the organisation of powers, the distribution of the places and roles, and the system of legitimising this distribution."[12] Contrary to that, politics is an activity that breaks up this unity of processes and interferes with the orderly configuration of the sensual. This makes politics profoundly linked to change; politics "is first and foremost a conflict regarding the scene in common, regarding the existence and status of those who are present there".[13] Although this difference, as established by philosophers when they want to think politically, could also be ascribed to the philosophical separation of the notion from its actuality in order to reveal its essence, this is not the main reason behind it.

This kind of differentiation between politics and the political itself – in order to return to its constitutive dimension – is also a consequence of something that is directly revealed to us through the speech act practice taking place in the film by the British artist Carey Young. It is not about living in a post-political world; this addition of *post-* actually springs from the considerably more difficult option of creating forms of reality through which communities are established. We cannot ignore the fact that the political effects people's communities. The simple fact that, when we want to talk about the political, the first problems we encounter are connected to language (in which we articulate political and life's ways of being), brings us to the problem discussed by Giorgio Agamben: the exploitation of life forms common to mankind establish the social conditions of capitalism. Agamben states that language is one of the basic forms of the communal. By means of language, people have always been able to realise themselves in terms of the truest path of human existence: they have been able to materialize their own essence as a possibility or potentiality.[14]

The inability to realise one's own essence as a possibility or potentiality, which springs from the exploitation of the forms of the communal that are most related to life, experiences its apotheosis in the democratic spectacle of organizing activity and interests. If we wish to think of the political in relation to art beyond the caesura and actually connect art with the essence of the political, then what primarily needs to be rethought is the post-political approach, where 'the political is truly in shape' or, we might even say, in vogue. This different approach is no longer just a consequence of the perspective that there is always something that needs to be deconstructed, e.g. the theatrical apparatus, the spectator or the context. Today, this protocol frequently comes across as politically ineffective, especially when we reflect on the political in the direction of insoluble antagonism. This means that we need to profoundly rethink the status of so-called critical art, which has become one of the most important ways for art to connect with forms of contemporary life and take political stances.

The critical art of today continues the active, progressive political role of avant-garde art without actually having a proper addressee. Art may provoke, show different views, warn and take critical stances, but there are few cases where it interferes with ways of being so radically that it can actually open up possibilities for life that lies ahead. It can be topical, but rarely does that topicality shatter the form through which it is established. According to Rancière, the relationship between politics and art is not a relationship between two separate partners. Art brings to politics what politics already contains: art makes visible the division of the sensible, an articulation of the political field that is closely connected to the being of the community.[15]

Here, we can agree with Rancière that politics does not consist of "relations of power, it consists of the relationships between worlds".[16] In this sense, the political subjectivisation that can take place in theatre, for instance, is not the recognition of the community as it already is, nor is it the recognition of those who are right or the recognition of things we have in common. Subjectivisation gives rise to a certain new multitude that calls for a different kind of enumeration. "Political subjectivisation divides anew the experiential field though which everyone's identity and share has been bestowed."[17] Every subjectivisation is therefore also a dis-identification, a painful and paradoxical process of being torn out of the place of the usual political order. The basic question on the relationship between art and politics is therefore that of the antagonistic and inevitable place of the communal, which concerns possible material and perceptive paths of life still to come. In this sense, art is firmly intertwined with questions concerning the conditions and possibilities of life itself; art interferes with the disclosure of potential modes of common realities. Art is therefore not articulated within the discursive contexts of self-referentiality and critical distance from its own self, but directly challenges and demolishes a colourful range of contexts in which it appears and becomes visible, and at the same time, does not consent to the reduction of art to a moral and didactic stance. The new political effect of art could therefore be sought "producing situations from the assumption that the capacity to act is larger than the pre-given institutional means to realize it; that the potentiality is really different from the possibility understood as opportunity in the institutional market."[18] This is why the continuation of this book will deal with various methods of artistic work; I am of the opinion that these methods are closely connected to the question of the political powerlessness or power of art. The question central to this book, is the following: how and what does art actually produce in contemporary capitalism?

Artist at Work, Proximity of Art and Capitalism

Studying the artist at work reveals many traits of the ambivalent closeness of art and capitalism. On the one hand, the work of the artist is at the core of capital speculations on art's value; on the other hand, by means of its work, art also resists the appropriation of its artistic powers. Artistic work is the focus of my interest because it allows us to analyse some important characteristics of the development of contemporary art in the last few decades and especially the changes in the forms of artistic autonomy that appeared with the increasing closeness of art and life. The aim of my book is therefore to note that these changes are closely connected to the changes in contemporary capitalism and the entry of post-Fordist ways of production into the centre of contemporary production.

Chapter 2

The Production of Subjectivity

2.1. The Crisis of Subjectivity

In an interview in which he critically revaluates the use of one of his key terms, 'immaterial labour', Maurizio Lazzarato states that, when describing the traits of contemporary capitalism, it is better to talk about the production of subjectivity rather than immaterial or cognitive labour. The production of subjectivity is at the core of capitalism, or as Lazzarato puts it, is actually its greatest effect – "the single largest commodity we produce, because it goes into the production of all other commodities."[19] Lazzarato's production of subjectivity hints at the standardisation of the social, affective and common aspects of the contemporary human being. These are at the core of production and essentially contribute to the creation of value. They result in a radical individualisation as well as a homogenisation of subjectivity; the production of the models of subjectivity is at the centre of capitalism. Contemporary society places great emphasis on creativity, imagination and dynamism, but these human powers have never before been as standardised and intertwined with what Foucault terms self-governance. Described by Franco Berardi Bifo as 'semiocapitalism', post-Fordist ways of working centre around thought, language and creativity as the primary tools for the production of value.[20] Experimentation with subjectivity (in terms of its imagination, creativity and time), the changed ways of working that bring work close to political activity (Virno), and the interiorisation of the microdynamics of power (Deleuze) are at the core of the contemporary generation of capitalist value. This thesis becomes especially interesting when applied to the development of contemporary art in the second half of the twentieth century, which takes place at the centre of the rebellion against the standardisation of modern life and the revaluation of the relationship between art and life. The contemporary status of art is highly controversial; it is closely connected to contemporary modes of the production of subjectivity, which makes it function as a creative, affective and social power that is becoming increasingly fused with other forms of creative production. At the same time, there is still a strong belief in the emancipatory and autonomous utopian power of art. It seems that the more political and socially engaged art is, the more it actually becomes isolated from its social and political power.

Since the second half of the twentieth century at least, the crisis of subjectivity has been at the centre of many emancipatory and experimental artistic practices – especially in performance, dance and visual art. It is not so much about the crisis of political subjectivity as it is about the establishment of new forms of the disintegrated, no longer hierarchically organised subject. Subjectivity is no longer established through an authentic core. We can no longer talk about a proportionate relationship between the subject's inside and outside; subjectivity turns outward as an empty process, a disintegrated structure of language and gesture (as e.g. by Beckett). Many experimental and neo-avant-garde practices are linked to Artaud's demand for a 'body without organs', which refers to a radical refusal of any kind of 'organisation' of organism.[21] At the same time, many artistic practices seem to be connected with Bataille's affirmation of negativity as a transformational force connecting the forces of becoming and the power of affirmation with negativity. The subject therefore frequently exists as a pulsating sum of various conflicting powers and forces. At its forefront are the negativity of becoming and the desiring dimension of power, which make it more of an assemblage of various traces and intensisites. In contemporary dance and performance, this loss of the subject's centre (where the subject no longer is the locus of truth) influences new creation procedures and the poetics of bodily and speech gestures. The crisis of subjectivity also radically interferes with the forms of embodiment on stage, shifting the origin of bodily motion to the outside and to everyday life, and opening the space of subjectivity to the experimentation with transformation and negativity. Such a crisis of subjectivity is also connected to another trait of art in recent decades – the increasing closeness of art and life, which shifts autonomy from the subject's interior to the exterior independence of the material processes of being, to the volatile flow of life and being.

The crisis of subjectivity becomes highly interesting in connection with production in contemporary capitalism, especially with the way in which experimenting with subjectivity is at the centre of capitalist production. The appearance of numerous critiques of art on account of its similarity to post-Fordist ways of working is not coincidental. What art and capitalism have especially in common is the dangerous and seductive closeness of the appropriation of life. In my opinion, many critiques that reflect on the similarity between art and capitalism overlook the central role of life and the role of experimentation with subjectivity in capitalism. The constant flexibility and transformation of the crisis of subjectivity are the central investing and consuming forces that drive the production of life. Today, the crisis of subjectivity has lost the emancipatory potential that it had in the artistic practices of the 1960s and 1970s, or at least needs to rethink and implement this potential in an entirely new manner. The main reason for this powerlessness is the fact that today's human being is confronted with a brutal intensification of individualisation processes, described by Lazzarato as the production of subjectivity. Old forms of life become obsolete even before they can actually be absorbed. This opens up the way for subjectivity, which experiences its transformation through constant existential paradoxes. This makes us live in a constant state of tension, at the edge of anxiety; it is this state that causes an increase in our investments. "Moreover, the process is intensified even further by the fact that this aggravated tension and speeded-up power of invention not only nourish capital but actually constitute its principal source of value, its most profitable investment."[22] The performance art and dance of the second half of the twentieth century often centred upon this 'radical consumption', the intense power of transformation through which the crisis of subjectivity enters the field of performance as a power, a force of negativity, and a conglomerate of affects and desires. In this context, I see radical consumption as the consumption of the body, presence, human actions and abilities, physical strength, spiritual power and affects; it aims to intervene into the intersubjective and productive nature of subjectivity and, in this way, also open up the relationship between performers and spectators. It drives the live communicative situations in contemporary performance beyond the conventional, established representations and powers of signification; this also holds for theatre interested in research into human energies, affects, the disclosure of new modes of acting and performativity (René Pollesch, Ivica Bujan, Rodrigo Garcia etc.). The live event therefore becomes a unique field for testing the effects of radical consumption, a field for practicing intersubjectivity, exchange and testing live communicative situations, for a rivet between the body and its expression (gesture, language, movement). This expression also points to the contemporary status of consumption as the main economic power that contemporary society and culture understand as an affirmative force of progress and success: the more we consume, the better off we'll be. According to Pfaller, contemporary consumption takes place in a very special way: we spend by not really enjoying it and constantly limit the excesses of life.[23] In this sense, today's consumption is a neurotic force. It offers us the illusion of endless transformation, but that transformation is without negativity – a standardised transformation of the subject. In the continuation, I therefore wish to argue that, in recent decades, a shift has taken place in the understanding of subjectivity and the status of radical consumption; this shift is connected to the social and cultural shifts of post-industrial capitalism. Subjectivity is at the core of methods of production and contemporary work processes. At the same time, consumption is becoming a negative force destroying the traditional common ways of being and life as such. In this sense, the relationship between art and the mechanisms of subjectivity need to be rethought since this would enable us to intervene in many interesting relations between art and politics.

Radical consumption in art is a consequence of the crisis of the subject, or that of the need for the visibility of the subject's constitution and split nature. Established through this visibility of the subject are the radical critique of essentialism and patriarchal structure of the subject. The visibility of the subject could also be described as a way of transgression and resistance to authenticity. The disclosure of the subject's negativity as a constitutive moment of subjectivisation has deeply marked the theatrical reforms of performing and ways of presence in performance art and live art. It also effects the formation of new spectator relations. However, it also constitutes the foundation of the 'emancipatory' power of art, especially its resistance to the rigid ways of contemporary life. In contemporary performance, the live event often becomes an opportunity for the radical consumption of the subject, an event without repetition[24], for a radical use of the body and a phenomenological blurring of the border between perception and the visible, the body and its edge. The potential power of the live event is often seen in this liberating power of negativity. This negativity not only breaks down the border between the stage and the spectator, but radically shifts the symbolic mandate of the actor and the spectator. It shatters the safe conventions within which the live artistic event is supposed to take place. The crisis of the subject is also at the core of acting reforms and research into how to embrace the consumption of the energy and power of acting, how to fight fake efficiency, open the intercommunicative potential of theatre and establish a split between presence and representation. The private, the intimate and the most hidden thus enter performance through the main entrance, but not as cheap exhibitionism (as strengthened by the low-end voyeurism on the other side). It is rather a rebellion against the rigid structures of power and a confrontation with the conventional apparatus of representation. The split within the subject namely becomes visible through the absence of equality between presence and representation, which is at the core of every subjectivisation process.[25]

When discussing this openness of the economy of looking and the dialectic of the pleasure of the spectator, this desiring participation that convinces us of the inter-subjectivity of performing, we should ask ourselves if this isn't something that exists as a more problematic side of the live event today. Doesn't performing the crisis of subjectivity cover up a basic commodification of the artistic event, the political powerlessness of performance, performance art and the body's action? In other words, do the radical actions of the body's rebellion against rigid power structures not make it succumb to power even more? It is not so much about radical consumption no longer filling us with strong affects, shame or disgust, i.e. about it stopping to disclose the desire on the part of the one watching. We can still be shocked, surprised and also exposed in our symbolic mandate of the spectator; we can still be called in what Erika Fischer-Lichte terms the 'feedback loop'.[26] Nevertheless, the potentiality of radical consumption seems to have been profoundly weakened; it appears to have lost the bowstring upon which its arrow was to rest. This strong affect, as well as the disclosure of desire and inter-subjectivity, are at the core of the contemporary structures of power – the methods of producing and controlling social relations. "The more diverse, even erratic, the better. Normality is losing its support. The regularities begin to loosen. This loosening of normality is part of the dynamics of capitalism. It is not simply about liberation. It is about the form of power/authority characteristic of capitalism. This is no longer a disciplinary institutional power/authority that determines everything, but power/authority in order to produce diversity – because markets get saturated. Even the weirdest affective tendencies are in order – as long as they bring money."[27]

This loosening of normality is problematic because, according to Massumi, there is a sort of relationship today between the dynamics of power and rebellion, where the strategies of rebellion can no longer be simply extracted. The exact opposite is taking place: the field of relationships between people, our ethical values, actions, desires, expectations, shameful bizarreness (no matter what pure expectations and possibilities it may be connected to), and desiring exchange – all this forms the surplus value of contemporary economics. Radical consumption (not in the sense of money but energy, human possibilities and actions) is at the core of the spirit of contemporary capitalism, where protestant asceticism has been replaced by the imperative of (ascetic) pleasure. The crisis of the subject thus reveals itself as an endless barrage of human abilities, actions and aspirations, the driving force of contemporary non-material production: one needs to be and constantly persist in a state of crisis in order to be even more creative. Today, consumption in art hardly seems to be a sign of liberation, a grand-scheme sensorial openness that would help us again place ourselves as subjects, because the tension we are supposed to resist no longer exists. In the continuation of the book, I will try to show that consumption itself should be read in a different way: the tension we need to resist is the one that regulates the lavish material artistic practices.

It seems that radical consumption directly gives rise to a new form of power – the power springing from the loosening and fluidity of our desires, or from the power arising from our need for liberation and transformation – from the imperative that we should be as shameless as possible in all of this. This ambivalent place of shame in relationship to radical consumption is shown quite convincingly by the performances of the Slovenian group Via Negativa. The performances by Via Negativa were created as part of a long-duration research project by the director Bojan Jablanovec; together with his performers, Jablanovec studies the acting strategies of presenting, ways of presence and creating new communicative relationships with the audience. The work by Via Negativa is chiefly subject to analyses concentrating on the dynamic of exchange and the role of the audience.

It seems to me that its work can also be viewed from a broader perspective – in the context of a wider economic exchange in which we participate day by day and where we are invited as desiring and 'investing' subjects.[28] Many performances by Via Negativa are radical yet cynical in nature and therefore do not give rise to emancipatory or inter-subjective effects; they cause uneasiness and provocation, but also a feeling of void or resignation concerning one's own passivity, sometimes also shame. Via Negativa's research namely employs the radical consumption of the subject and the body (with its fluids, openings, physical exhaustion, repetitiveness, mental concentration) in the forms of confession, using them as a strategy to achieve inter-communication and a shift of the function of the spectator. In this sense, Via Negativa consistently follows performance art practices or phenomenological destruction of the live event; placed into the centre are the body and the shaping of the subject as a means of dealing with the availability and achievement of affective reactions. Consumption does not really have a concrete place in Via Negativa's research; it is rigid, unsuccessful and empty, as though it were clear in advance that the selected strategy would not have an effect. At the moment it could become 'something' its every meaning and purpose is abolished. The works by Via Negativa organise and literally perform the mechanisms of subjectivisation, which directly connects them with the questions on the relationship between subjectivisation and contemporary production, with issues of the role of the processes of subjectivisation in contemporary capitalism. At the same time, their works constantly profane every excess of the spectator's or actor's investment; frequently, the consumption of acting or performance energies purposely leave little more left than what actually happens; the consumption does not have a symbolic justification.

A further trait of these performance art pieces is that they frequently revolve around a confession, especially in the first part of their research, focussing on the seven capital vices. The results of their research project are presented in the form of short performances as a series of confessions; their point of utterance is always the individuality of each participating actor or actress. It is also important that the utterance never remains at the level of speech: everything that is uttered triggers a real action. The truths uttered by the participants about themselves and their work are performances because the language of the confession not only describes reality but also establishes and changes it. The truths uttered by the participants are therefore not existentialist in nature. Their 'reality' only shows itself though action; it is a result of the intertwining of verbal and non-verbal actions. At the same time, however, the truths uttered by the participants are not essentialist truths; their 'real character' only becomes apparent through action, as a result of the intertwinement of verbal and non-verbal actions on stage. This does not mean that the confession and action are harmonious in the relationship between cause and effect. It is more about a radical alienation of speech and action, the establishment of an empty place where the performance art of the person can be established.[29] Interestingly, what is confessed is often not only an intimate fact, but also closely connected to the work performed by the person confessing: with acting or performance 'labour', and indirectly also with theatre as the point of utterance. The subject's hunt for the real is paradoxically framed into the (public) work performed by the participants in the scenes, who simultaneously admit its shortcomings. We seem to witness a public form of 'penitence', a contemporary version of the flagellates. We can only participate if we are also ready to accept the abominable dregs of the real (the medium of spoken confession is namely the body with its fluids and openings), and thus confess our own obscene pleasure. But the confession in the Via Negativa project is not only a way of pointing out the voyeuristic economy of the spectator's exchange and pleasure, where the actor's body and action are established as those of a victim in order for us to be able to see or in order for the obscene to surface. The Via Negativa project does not stop at moralism, but sharpens the theatrical situation into a dispositif of public subjectivisation. Their works are organised. In other words, they literally perform the mechanisms of subjectivisation, which directly connect them with questions on the relationship between subjectivisation and contemporary production. Especially if we consider that we frequently work today by performing our own selves. In a way, we all are actors in the way we work, while work is increasingly becoming public. We can therefore also view the performances by Via Negativa as research into the role of the processes of subjectivisation in contemporary capitalism. An important trait of the contemporary way of working is the consumption of subjectivity, the only way of opening the chance for us to produce even more.[30]

Foucault writes that as the dispositif of subjectivisation (i.e. the manner in which the subject is established and its singularity articulated), confession entered Western culture already in the nineteenth century, when it replaced the classic dispositif of remorse by new forms of power and ruling. "We have since become a singularly confessing society. The confession has spread its effects far and wide. It plays a part in justice, medicine, education, family relationships, and love relations, in the most ordinary affairs of everyday live, and in the most solemn rites; one confesses one's crimes, one's sins, one's thoughts and desires, one's illnesses and troubles; one goes about telling, with the greatest precision, whatever is most difficult to tell. One confesses in public and in private, to one's parents, one's educators, one's doctor, to those one loves; one admits to oneself, in pleasure and in pain, things it would be impossible to tell anyone else, the things people write books about. One confesses–or is forced to confess."[31] Confession is something that does not come from the outside as a consequence of the subject's discipline, but is actually the governance over the subject's inside by the subject themselves; it becomes part of the techniques of self-control and self-governance, so characteristic of the functioning of contemporary power. Confessions are often made in art as well. Today, confession has become a way of producing truth: truth can only become visible or come to the surface by means of confession. Truth will out, and if it fails to reveal itself, one needs to get rid of the limitations that prevent this from happening. Only by means of confession can we establish our singularity, in which the following essential rule must be observed: I must incessantly utter what is hardest to say. In order to achieve that, I need to feel confession as a deeply personal, intimate need. Foucault writes that this need and obligation to confess have been so deeply internalized that we no longer feel it as an effect of power. It is no longer felt as an effect of dominance, but becomes a deep intimate need – proof that we are capable of changing. Foucault connects the need to confess with the analysis of the new forms of power and control, which are no longer connected to traditional disciplining techniques but make use of refined forms of self-control, which could also be termed self-governance. His analysis is still quite topical, especially given the various forms of subjectivisation available to us as users of and workers in today's labour market. We are subjects that are continuously capable of transforming, exhausting and selling the most intimate within us (for this is where our essence is supposed to lie). As Peter Klepec finds, we always need to be free enough to make confessions, feel confession as our innermost need, and at the same time be shameless and flexible enough to reject and utterly profane the very truth we have reached and disclosed with such great difficulty. If we constantly utter what is hardest to say, then what is told is no longer of particular secrecy.[32]

It is not unusual today for confession to be turned into a media spectacle; it is not so much about 'cheap' spectacle and uninformed voyeuristic spectators, but about a radical change in the manner of controlling and shaping contemporary subjectivity. Confession is not a disclosure where someone shows themselves as they really are, but a mechanism of subordination and part of the flexible subjectivisation enabled by contemporary society and its numerous dispositives (of a technological, political and economic nature). Today, our surplus lies primarily in the fact that we are subjects about whom something new can always be discovered; we constantly need to reveal and topicalise our potential abilities. "The statement 'you lack potential' is much more devastating than 'you messed up.' It makes a more fundamental claim about who you are. It conveys uselessness in a more profound sense."[33]

There is another important trait framing Via Negativa's artistic work into highly topical contradictions of subjectivisation and pointing out the problematic status of the radical consumption of the performer. The confessions uttered by the performers and triggering scenes/actions are closely connected to the work they do – to the expectations and social/professional status of the persons/actors speaking, almost to certain 'professional ethics'. The sinfulness or research of human weaknesses can be connected to the classical findings of Max Weber about a rational lifestyle, based on the idea of profession and the spirit of capitalism, which puts one's "professional duty"[34] first. This profoundly changes our relationship to the hidden and the intimate: it is no longer about the dark sinfulness of our untameable flesh, but about any kind of secrecy related to professional asceticism, to the imperative of work; in this, human weakness is regarded as a consequence of the irrational consumption of property. The cardinal vice in the ideal of professional asceticism is therefore that of the void of consumption of human abilities and actions. What needs to be added to this realisation is an important characteristic of the present time, or of current social relations. Today, professional asceticism, the active realisation of the human will in professions (as discussed by Weber), has been replaced by the imperative of 'professional' enjoyment. Now, we must incessantly consume human abilities and actions. If we wish to work successfully, we must come across as relaxed as possible, babble as much as possible, be as shameful, flexible and creative as possible, enjoy and show all of our potentiality and be critical to boot. Furthermore, we must do this publicly because contemporary work increasingly takes place before the eyes of another.

In this sense, the performer becomes the ideal virtuoso worker of contemporary capitalism, producing 'communication through the means of communication'; the means are the language and actions of the body. This claim can also be connected to the disappearance of the differences between various kinds of human activity – work, political activity and intellect as described by Virno, who also points out that our manner of working today is the same as that of politicians. We work with our own communication means and before the eyes of others (publicly), i.e. by performing for others. The fact that work is political also means that work becomes performative – it takes place through communication and speech acts.[35] We work by means of our affective, intimate, communicational and human powers whose transformation and flexibility must always be performance-oriented; they need to have an effect. It is therefore no coincidence that, in recent years, the use of the word 'performer' has been increasingly used in place of 'actor' or 'dancer'. The term 'performer' is supposed to have a wider, more interdisciplinary nature, not limited in advance in terms of the 'technical' knowledge of individual genres, which enables a more liberal naming of the activity. However, the performer is also skilled at a specific technique – the self-performing or radical consumption of their own powers for the processes of the constant transformation of bodily states and affective powers. Herein lies the core of the cynicism that underlies the tasks of the actors and performers in the aforementioned Via Negativa scenes, as well as our own attitude to the actions performed. Radical senseless consumption is also a reflection of the expected excess of transformation that does not take place. The work that drives us to 'go into ourselves fully and completely', both socially and artistically, actually produces nothing of value. This results in a radically failed subjectivisation, powerlessness and impotent promises that are never realised. This radical failure can be connected to the production of subjectivity in capitalism: the more we are invited to be creative, political, revolutionary and dynamic in our ways of working, the more standardised and controlled our subjectivity becomes; our only freedom becomes that of utter individuality, which can be selected in the market of homogenously individualised offers.

2.2. Problems with Profanation

Contemporary forms of subjectivisation are also discussed by Giorgio Agamben. In one of his short essays, he sets the hypothesis that desubjectivisation is at the heart of today's crisis of the subject. For Agamben, the subject is always a result of the relationship between living beings and dispositives, in which the dispositif – as a conglomerate of practices, tasks, processes, inclusions and exclusions – must always imply some process of subjectivisation; without subjectivisation, the dispositif would be sheer violence.[36] Agamben defines the dispositif (apparatus) as "literarlly anything that has in some way the capacity to capture, orient, determine, intercept, model, control, or secure the gestures, behaviours, opinions or discourses of living beings."[37] Interestingly, Agamben compares the structure of the dispositif to the dispositif of remorse, which brings us back to the topic of confession: the need for the disclosure of the subject (necessary for it to become the subject at the core of early modern subjectivisation). Agamben writes that there is always a double dynamic at work in the dispositif. In the case of remorse, the new self is constituted through negation; at the same time, the negation allows it to get the old self back again. The subject thus needs to split in order to be able to find its truth and become a subject. In Agamben's terms: the subject finds its truth in the non-truth of its sinful self. This brings us back to the crisis of the subject, which Agamben defines as the distinction that takes place through every constituting of the subject. As already mentioned, this distinction, the disclosure of the presence in this point of distinction, crisis and tension, represents an important part of the history of performance art. In this way, the live event forms new dispositifs of observing, which make us direct witnesses to the subjectivisation process. Performance art often affirms itself as a sort of open negativity, the emancipatory power of differentiation and transformation; for this reason, negativity always produces some sort of symbolic surplus, however disgusting and repulsive it may be. The fact that this potentiality of negativity nowadays shows itself as something problematic, or as something radically powerless and completely commodified, is a misunderstanding, and can be ascribed to what Agamben defines as a change in the dispositifs we deal with in the current phase of capitalism. It is necessary to go one step further and say that, today dispositives "no longer act as much through the production of a subject, as through the processes of what can be called desubjectification."[38] What actually happens is that the two processes, subjectivisation and desubjectivisation, abolish the difference between them; since there is no more distinction, the place of recomposition of the new subject becomes lost. "In the non-truth of the subject, its own truth is no longer at stake."[39]

If applied to the history of radical consumption in art, Agamben's finding effects the accepted narrative and understanding of performance art as an artistic form. Performance art has always been about the process (of subjectivisation, objectivisation, etc.); something happens or shifts. As spectators, we literally enter the split and by entering it, we are addressed as subjects. Due to changes in the ways that the networks of practices, manners and actions direct subjectivisation nowadays (i.e. the changes resulting from the fact that today's daily human actions, ways and practices are becoming the driving force of contemporary production), the dispositifs are forever multiplied. According to Agamben, they are also accompanied by excessive proliferation of subjectivisation processes. We live in a time of endless choices between subjectivities, identities and opportunities; at the same time however, subjectivity seems to profoundly elude us. Despite the vastly increasing number of dispositives through which we can establish ourselves as subjects, even the most common of our daily activities are controlled by these processes, which, paradoxically, give us the freedom of realizing ourselves. Although we are driven by strong desire, we do not acquire subjectivity, only a new form of control. Let us go back to theatre and the powerlessness of radical consumption: have the numerous contemporary ways of subjectivisation and the diversity and flexibility of the market of contemporary subjectivities not radically delineated the choice of practices in a live event, or radically narrowed its political and transgressive potentiality? Isn't the powerlessness of the action in art precisely in this blockade (constant desubjectivisation) of contemporary ways of being – this expansion of the masquerade of actualisation of everything we do – and accompanies us in our daily and professional lives?

Any utterance is closely connected to subjectivisation; when we speak up, we get subjectivised and subordinated at the same time; through speech, we get our action from the power we resist.[40] Agamben finds that, in contemporaneity, the dynamics of subordination and establishment aggravates because the division between the processes of subjectivisation and desubjectivisation disappears. What remains is 'non-violent subordination', a voluntary slavery where no subjectivity can be acquired. These new ways of subjectivisation also have a completely different connection to profanation, which Agamben defines as a procedure by means of which "what was captured and divided by means of apparatuses, is set free and returned to common use."[41] Agamben connects his reflections on profanation with the role of religion, which he defines as "what detaches things, places, people, animals and persons from the common use and transports them to a separate sphere."[42] Profanation therefore means the returning of these things to common use and can also be understood as the "anti-apparatus that restores to common use what sacrifice has separated and divided."[43] Profanation is a powerful procedure because it neutralises what it profanes; it takes the aura away from things and people. Profanation is a highly important procedure in twentieth century art and is deeply inscribed in the paradoxical relationship between art and life. Art is thereby established as a sort of field of radical events, a field of the potentiality of rebelling against the rigid structures of contemporary life; art also enables the autonomy of the artistic object. It is the political process that triggers inter-subjectivity in the performance; phenomenological openness is only possible if something is in common use, if it is exempt from separation. We need to consider a radical change in contemporary life concerning the potentiality of profanation as the process of returning things to common use. Agamben namely points out that we live in a time of profoundly changed dispositives as processes of desubjectivisation, which makes the profanation procedures so much more difficult. Capitalism establishes itself as the sort of system that, in its final stage, becomes a system for embracing all profane behaviours (transgression, rebellion, negativity, provocation, radical consumption, etc.). In this sense, capitalism is a religion targeting the absolutely 'non-profanable'; in its extreme form, capitalism embodies "the pure form of separation, without anything left to separate. Absolute profanation, which has no residue, henceforth coincides with a kind of consecration, which is equally empty and integral."[44] It is not a coincidence that Agamben sees the realisation of this dream of the absolutely non-profanable in the most profane: pornography. Pornography could be denoted as the ultimate trait of production; indeed, the most active (current) form of capitalism comes across as utterly obscene.

Profane problems are also discussed by the philosopher Peter Klepec, who states that profanation has become impossible, or better put, that this gesture requires special procedures nowadays.[45] If we connect this premise with contemporary art, especially with the potentiality of radical consumption, we are faced with a deep problem as far as radical experience in art is concerned. This feeling is further strengthened by the fact that, today, procedures of artistic profanation exist as objects of value (e.g. many body art and performance art documents constitute an important part of numerous contemporary art collections, with performance art stepping into the mainstream artistic market on a grand scale). "A perplexing phenomenon has occurred in the past seven years: the blob of the mainstream has devoured the lingo and imagery of the much touted 'margin' – the thornier and more sharp-edged, the better – and 'performance' has literally turned into a sexy marketing strategy and pop genre. I call this phenomenon the 'mainstream bizarre.'"[46] There is also a parallel entry of radical experience into the museum. According to Agamben, today, the museum is not a given physical space or place, but "the separate dimension to which what was once – but is no longer – felt as true and decisive has moved."[47] The museum is therefore the sacred space where something has sought refuge that was once felt as real; there is no possibility of use, being and experience. The museum is therefore the space where profane artistic procedures are isolated and given an almost ritualistic character, again returning to the field of the sacred rather than the common. We can therefore observe the deterritorialisation of spaces of obscenity and the fact that, today, there are new divorces taking place between the common and what is taken out of the common and placed upon display. In my opinion, this is closely connected to new forms of subjectivity, where experimentation and the crisis of the subject drive the production of signs and gestures, which shifts the values about the importance of artistic gestures. These new values can best be analysed using examples of change in the work of the performer.

2.3. The Work of the Performance Artist

A good example of the fact that the production of subjectivity (and consequently its exploitation) is at the core of contemporary culture can be found in an interesting conflict between two 'matrons' of the performance and experimental art of the second half of the twentieth century, which took place in the autumn of 2011 and immediately became viral news on numerous social networks. The case reveals many paradoxes surrounding the contemporary social and cultural role of performance art and body art, as well as the complex role of performance art in contemporary capitalism.

In 2011, Marina Abramović was invited to collaborate as guest artist at the Los Angeles Museum Gala, considered one of the most prestigious events in contemporary visual art. The evening is primarily conceived as a dinner with the museum donors; every year, it is co-designed by an artistic or pop-culture celebrity. The event is quite well-known and notorious, especially in recent years, with many popular stars having collaborated as guests (e.g. Lady Gaga, Angelina Jolie and Brad Pitt, etc.). In 2011, the honour was bestowed upon Marina Abramović; as creative director of the event; she also invited the singer Debbie Harry. Individual seats at the gala dinner cost between 25,000 and 100,000 USD, with the proceeds also used as a donation to the museum. Abramović has recently prepared a number of grand-scale revivals and reconstructions of her performance art pieces (the most well-known is the exhibition/event *The Artist is Present*, MOMA, New York, 2010). For the gala dinner, she organized an audition to select the performers for a reconstruction of her work *Nude with Skeleton* (2002) and other performative actions that were to take place. Over 800 people applied, of which 'only' 200 were invited to audition. Some of those auditioning declined to collaborate subsequently. One of them notified the well-known American choreographer and video artist Yvonne Rainer on her reasons for this. Together with art critic Douglas Crimp and visual artist Taisha Paggett, Rainer wrote an indignant letter of protest to the museum director Jeffrey Deitch. The letter criticized the collaboration conditions at the event and denoted them as exploitive: "Ms Abramović is so wedded to her original vision that she – and by extension, the Museum director and curators – don't see the egregious associations for the performers, who, though willing, will be exploited nonetheless. Their desperate voluntarism says something about the generally exploitative conditions of the art world such that people are willing to become decorative table ornaments installed by a celebrity artist in the hopes of somehow breaking into show biz themselves. And at sub-minimal wages for the performers, the event is economic exploitation as well, verging on criminality."[48] Rainer's information source was the choreographer and dancer Sarah Wookey.

Several days after the reaction of Rainer and her colleagues, Wookey revealed her identity in an open letter describing her role in the event in more detail, as well as the reasons that led to her decision to decline to collaborate: "I refused to participate as a performer because what I anticipated would be a few hours of creative labour, a meal, and the chance to network with like-minded colleagues turned out to be an unfairly remunerated job. I was expected to lie naked and speechless on a slowly rotating table, starting from before the guests arrived and lasting until after they left (a total of nearly four hours). I was expected to ignore (by staying in what Abramović refers to as 'performance mode') any potential physical or verbal harassment while performing. I was expected to commit to fifteen hours of rehearsal time, and sign a Non-Disclosure Agreement stating that if I spoke to anyone about what happened in the audition I was liable for being sued by Bounce Events, Marketing, Inc., the event's producer, for a sum of $1 million dollars plus attorney fees. I was to be paid $150."[49]

Wookey's letter describes some of the expected tasks of the performers; some were to sit under the round dinner tables on small revolving chairs, with their heads peeking out of openings on the table, and turn among the cutlery, food and plates. They were to do that for three hours and strive to make eye contact with the guests seated at the table. At the audition, there was no mention of any protection for the performers nor any possible assistance to those who may have found themselves in trouble performing this live and certainly strenuous work.

The reaction of Marina Abramović and the organizers to the letter was huge and rather hurt. Abramović accused Rainer of being unfamiliar with the full context of the event, writing a letter of protest without experiencing the event, and putting herself demagogically on the side of the performers; many of them supposedly enjoyed the event and did not have any problems with the collaboration conditions. In a discussion with Harvard University students (Graduate School of Design), Abramović stated in a rather distressed manner that it had been highly unjust of Rainer to accuse her of exploitation as a daughter of a partisan and Yugoslav general, someone characterized by a strong communist background. Abramović also attacked Rainer for her supposed narrow-mindedness in terms of failing to see the critical or ironical stance of the event toward the donors. At the hall entrance, the guests had to put on white laboratory coats, covering up their shiny expensive clothes; they were also in an ambivalent situation due to their live contact with the performers. Their social and financial position was supposed to be rendered ironic through the role they played in the event.[50] Indeed, the footage of the event looks like that of a bizarrely aestheticised feast, a laboratory excess almost, where the blowout of the rich intertwines with the sweet cakes/corpses and living heads on the tables. For this reason, Rainer compares this event to *Salo* (1976), a controversial film by Pasolini, dealing with sadism and the sexual abuse of a group of adolescents by post-war Fascists; she makes this comparison with severe reservations however: "Reluctant as I am to dignify Abramović by mentioning Pasolini in the same breath, the latter at least had a socially credible justification tied to the cause of anti-fascism."[51]

A *New York Times* reporter described Abramović's event at the Moca (Museum of Contemporary Art) as an 'epic gala evening'. More epic than the evening itself is the battle of two twentieth century experimental art icons. It reveals some essential traits of the closeness of art and capitalism, which also underlies the new culturally and politically complex situation of contemporary performance art. Today, there are differences present in the work of performance artists, with their bodies and enduring subjectivity at its very core. This brings us back to the previous chapter and the interesting status of the performer's work, which can be closely associated with the changes of work in contemporary capitalism. This battle is therefore not a syndicalist one (i.e. pertaining to an adequate remuneration for the work in question), but it would also be too narrow to understand it as a moralist discussion on the appropriation of life and radical art by spectacular and globally-oriented artistic institutions (which is generally too frequent a target of critiques nowadays). We must delve further than the moralistic discussion on exploitation – in terms of who exploits the body in a more efficient manner: dancers (as Rainer was later reproached by Abramović) or performers, who offer their quiet, enduring subjectivity to create the atmosphere of the event?

There are quite a few problems at the core of this dispute that shatter the political power of performance art and indicate the capitalization of the artistic powers in contemporary culture. We can also connect this discussion with a now historical dilemma of avant-garde art, triggered by Yvonne Rainer's famous manifesto *No to spectacle* (1962); which influenced an entire generation of minimalist artists, especially in the US.

There is an interesting *déjà vu* to this dispute and it needs to be understood as a repetition of the difference of the same. With its consumption of the body, energy, human actions and presence, as well as with its encouragement of intersubjective exchange between the performance artist and performers, performance art has become a place of experimenting with subjectivity and life or their consumption through numerous political, sexual, discursive and cultural inscriptions. In the 1970s, performance art entered the centre of political and critical art. Live art challenged the institutional frames of art and exhibition, raising numerous questions on the representation of the body and gender, as well as the ideological and discursive constellations of the body. But how are we to view such artistic practices today, when subjectivity is at the core of human production (Lazzarato) and capital powers deeply affect the powers and potentialities of life?

The establishment of performance modes (Abramović) or atmospheres, affects, persistances, presences, intensities and tensions, can be thought of as performing human and subjective powers: these powers are at the centre of contemporary post-Fordist production. It must not be overlooked that such artistic practices take place at a time when human sociality is at the core of production and when our cognitive, affective and flexible abilities are part of the production of value; they are something that fuels contemporary capitalism. In view of the radical consumption of subjectivity, we can no longer avoid the issue of the labour performed by the (performance) artist in various contexts; his/her power or readiness to be 'present' is not just an immaterial aesthetic state, but is firmly connected to new manners of production and exploitation. Bodily or eventful states, atmospheres and intensities cannot be thought about without their social and political contexts; they do not exist as isolated art material because they are already deeply intertwined with numerous social and economic processes. The problem is therefore that in today's capitalism, we work in the manner that Abramović calls performance mode. One's work is intertwined with the performing and maintenance of creativity; in this, one should ignore every disturbance from the environment or political context, as well as any antagonist disturbance that comes from the sphere of the public.[52] We work with our language, imagination and creative abilities, but not in a manner that would lead to changes in the public sphere. The work in performance mode is therefore strongly depoliticized; our powers are separated from their practical and social contexts. Exploitation is therefore not only connected to the problematizing of the amount of payment for the work itself in the sense that the exploitation would have ceased if the performers had been sufficiently remunerated. It is primarily connected with the fact that Abramović's proposal exploits the very presence of the performers, their affective, direct and live persistence/endurance, in which the endurance of the bodies does not produce any public (political) effect, except contributing to the spectacular value of the artist and the institution she is supported by. At the centre of this work is their strain, a strain without a voice – their pure presence, robbed of any context. The performers are there as subjects without voices and clothing, or, as stated by Sarah Wookey in the letter she published a few days after Rainer's: "I would rather be the face of the outspoken artist than the silenced, slowly rotating head (or, worse, 'centre piece') at the table. I want a voice, loud and clear. Abramović's call for artists was, as the LA Times quoted, for 'strong, silent types.' I am certainly strong but I am not comfortable with silence in this situation. I refuse to be a silent artist regarding issues that affect my livelihood and the culture of my practice."[53]

The essential difference could lie in the fact that the beginnings of performance art in the second half of the twentieth century constituted a demand; the consumption of subjectivity was a way for the performance artist to demand their voice – a political and embodied voice –, and brought about an exchange with the sexual, social and political voices of the artists and disembodied institutional power. This is why the greatest part of the artists' work was not delegated; their lives and presence were not to serve celebrities – in other words, it was not work for someone else, as for example is the case of the spectacular reconstructions of performance art pieces in recent years.

This loss of voice is also quite close to the contemporary ways of working; those can also be revolutionary works without a political voice, with art and contemporary creative work closely resembling each other in this aspect.[54] This loss of voice also underlies the problematic loss of the critical and political power of performance art; this loss is not a consequence of appropriation by institutions that are supposed to make spectacles out of performance art pieces, but of a basic shift in the power and force of subjectivity. Today, subjectivity mostly comes across as produced, with subjectivity experimentation desired in the core of the contemporary capitalist spectacle.[55] It is in this sense that Rainer's reply entails the repetition of the same as the repetition of difference. Today, the repeated No to spectacle! can be read as a repeated No to spectacle! in art, a spectacle excessively ubiquitous in the artistic institutions of the contemporary world, which are related closely to capitalism. It speaks about the powerlessness of the profanation procedures in contemporary culture (as already discussed in the previous chapter).

In her Harvard University discussion, Abramović talks about Rainer not recognising the critical point of her work, which was a cynical stance towards the donors who showed up to attend the exclusive expensive gala dinner that evening. Abramović's fellow conversationalist, the art critic Sanford Kwinter agreed too, saying that Rainer's reaction reminded him of a similar scandal in 1974, when the *Artforum* newspaper published a photograph of Lynda Benglis on its front page. The artist was featured naked, with sunglasses and a large latex dildo. The photograph, which was actually an advertisement for Benglis's exhibition at the Paula Cooper Gallery, gave rise to numerous indignant reactions, including on the editorial board of the newspaper itself; in the next issue, Rosalind Krauss and other editorial board members described the cover as exploitive and brutal. Many other artists also recognised it as a gesture of the appropriation and commercialisation of art. A response to that was the founding of the still influential *October* magazine, founded in 1976 by two former members of the *Artforum* editorial board, Rosalind Krauss and Annette Michelson. In his conversation with Abramović, Kwinter stated that Rainer's reaction was reminiscent of puritan America – the puritanism and moralism deeply present in American avant-garde practices. In Kwinter's opinion, the reaction was connected to a puritanism that patronizingly condemns the pleasure and excess of art as well as their entry into the mainstream, taking away the critical point. Kwinter therefore considers Rainer's letter as a repetition of this 1970s event, as a puritanical reaction to the entry of radical and experimental art into mainstream culture. This repetition series can also be interpreted differently; it could be connected with a series of political differences placed by avant-garde art throughout the twentieth century into a kind of genealogy, which I will attempt to briefly sum up at this point.

In her 1962 manifesto, Rainer reacts to the excess and commodification of art, to the seduction of the spectator, offering the minimalism of art as a response. In the mid-1970s, the *October* magazine reacts to this commodification with an empty cover, opening the magazine to post-modernism, which only later starts to be reflected on in connection with post-Fordist manners of production and neoliberal cultural dynamics as well. In 2011, Rainer and like-minded individuals react to the exploitation of artistic work; after the end of the first decade of the twenty first century, this exploitation is at the core of producing spectacular value of the performance presence. Rainer thus discloses the closeness of art and capitalism. At the end of this chapter, this strategically created genealogy can yield at least two interesting conclusions.

The first is connected to the puritanism of the avant-garde; rather than moralising, it should actually be read as a demand for a reduction of artistic gestures and means. It testifies to the fact that all these repetitions can be read as demands for art that can be placed close to the contexts of the Russian historical avant-garde, discussed by Boris Groys. Nowadays, the avant-garde is frequently denoted as powerless, as the provocation of art is generated in close connection with capitalism, which places a further added value upon such procedures; for this reason, avant-garde art is supposed to be heavily commodified. Groys points out that it is not provocation, criticism, cynicism or striving for excess that is at the centre of the avant-garde; quite the opposite; avant-gardes are actually very ascetic practices, with the radical reduction and negation of procedures at their core.[56] It would be good to think about how the radical negation of procedures and artistic gestures can influence the creation of art today and reveal the power of art in terms of thinking the unthinkable, referring to the non-existent activity outside capitalised time. Such an interpretation helps us think of reduction separately from moralism and puritanism (where any kind of reduction and demand for 'less' is made by the contemporary culture of pleasure). It helps us connect artistic gesture with consistency, the procedures of profanation and the persistence of artistic life that does not drown in the excess of the real or in everything that art needs to address (especially if it aims to be political).

There is also a second conclusion that can be drawn from this genealogy of repetitions. The repetition in the dispute between Rainer and Abramović points out a trait of contemporary culture, a strange intertwinement between contemporary commodification and pleasure (enjoyment), which cannot take place in any other way than on demand. As mentioned above, the critical point of the radical consumption of the body gets lost in the age of the endless consumption of the body and energies, with the aim of producing even more. The critical point of this event is isolated; as stated in Rainer's letter, Abramović does not actually have an addressee or an aim (contrary to Pasolini) to direct herself at; the aim is therefore only a further establishment of the market value of the artist herself – that of the speculative expectation invested upfront in her position as an artist. Such an event is created within the existing system of art, which creates networks between excessively rich individuals and star artists, between rich investors and artistic works, between spectacular events and politically oriented curators. In this system, charitable people have a similar status as within the wider context of capitalism. Their position is analysed by Slavoj Žižek in his book *Violence*; in the chapter The Good Men from Porto Davos. He states that charity actually neutralises the chase for profit: "Charity is the humanitarian mask hiding the face of economic exploitation."[57] In this sense, the "sovereign self-negating gesture of the endless acquisition of wealth is to spend this wealth for things beyond price, and outside market circulation: public goods, art and sciences, health, etc."[58] According to Žižek, this is a way for the capitalists' life to acquire purpose; it is no longer just about widespread reproduction that is self-serving. In this way, the capitalist acquires public recognition; it is not only about satisfaction on the personal level; charity is "the logical concluding point of capitalistic circulation, necessary from the strictly economic standpoint, since it allows the capitalist system to postpone its crisis. It re-establishes balance – a kind of redistribution of wealth to the truly needy".[59] But what happens with capitalists who donate their wealth to art and receive tickets to the performance art pieces of the rich, in which they not only participate, but are also critically addressed? Their pleasure lies in the critical attitude towards them; it is in the co-existence of their status as the rich and a parodic critique of their role. This reflects the fact that the art of today is no longer capable of ridiculing its patrons because this is precisely what they expect from it; this is part of the excess value of their gift – the critical self-awareness and making fun of their own selves in front of everyone's eyes. Their pleasure must be provocative, ill-at-ease and unusual. Such charitable donors are sitting ducks for provocative actions directed at them; their status is that of the publicly admitted uneasiness that they constantly express by making donations to various institutions while making even more money themselves; these patrons are well aware that art will reveal this uneasiness without consequences. In this sense, capitalism and art meet at the point where art is isolated from any kind of symbolic power and participates in the flood of the real, obscene pleasure of those who financially support it. The fact that the guests need to ascetically cover up their clothes at the gala dinner just confirms that the asceticism of today is at work at the core of the greatest pleasure; at the centre of the most intense consumerism, there is control and discipline, the order to 'enjoy yourself!'.

The absence of the symbolic in the flood of real pleasure is also pointed out in Lacan's lecture that predicts the beginning of a new contemporary power: "The regime puts you on display; it says 'Watch them fuck'..."[60] His statement predicts the emergence of power based on the imperative of pleasure, gobbling up all rebellious and profane activities by means of new forms of subtle control and self-regulation. Lacan makes this statement in the scope of the lecture at the University of Vincennes in Paris, at the peak of the student and sexual revolution (1969) when the body, pleasure and the body's desires become the key fields of rebellion. "We see very rarely, this needs to be said, that someone dies of shame,"[61] Lacan says at the beginning of the lecture, one taking place at the height of elation, at the rise of relaxed and liberated post-industrial culture. He namely detects an interesting trait of this new culture of the liberated body, relaxed atmosphere, the new culture of consumerism and pleasure – in short, the culture of the liberated subject: this culture attempts to make shame disperse and vanish. This is why Lacan says to the students at the end of his lecture that a good reason, if any, for the lecture being so crowded should be sought in the fact that he arouses shame in them every now and then.

This syntagm should not be understood as a complaint by a conservative professor who classifies the current tumultuous goings-on in society as obscure and reacts to them in an aristocratic manner. The matter at hand is a lot more fundamental; this 'reservation', 'nobility', discretion (as termed by Žižek[62]) or 'honour' (as discussed by J. A. Miller) is actually in a radical dialogue with culture; insofar as culture abolishes shame, this is due to a radical change in the governing discourse. "Today, we are namely in a period when the ruling discourse forbids us to be ashamed of our pleasure any longer. Of everything else yes. Of our desire, but not of our pleasure."[63] Furthermore, shame is a performative process, an interesting affect that "effaces itself; shame points and projects; shame turns itself skin side out; shame and pride, shame and dignity, shame and self-display, shame and exhibitionism are different interlinings of the same glove."[64] Or, as stated by Alenka Zupančič: "Shame is the affect of the fact that we have not died of shame in a certain situation. This inner doubling of shame is the key point for the understanding of its essential dimension. In the not-to-die-of-shame situation, the subject is forced to see the downfall of his or her own signifier, the downfall of his or her own symbolic dimension. Although I am ashamed, I do not die along with my symbolic role."[65] If we apply this to the imperative of contemporary shameless culture, we can again see that the absence of shame exists due to the suppression of this symbolic dimension: nothing can be profaned any longer because everything has already been profaned.

For this reason, the letter by Sarah Wookey and Yvonne Rainer should also be understood as a repetition of the rebellion against the particular social role of art, as a demand for the voice of the artistic precariat, a demand for work performed by subjectivity and the body to be valued fairly. In this case, art does not yield to the existing state, but understands the consumption of subjectivity especially in terms of addressing its symbolic role in contemporary society, which is increasingly veiled by the reality of its work. It points out the public character of the artistic action and the ways in which any kind of work (no matter how quiet) is part of the constellations of power, the placement of social hierarchies and the demand for visibility in the public sphere. It also points out that there is a profound need in today's art to revalue artistic work and simultaneously preserve the power of the artistic procedures of profanation and experimenting as separate from the profane pleasures of the elite.

Chapter 3

The Production of Sociality

3.1. The Glut of Sociality

In 2011, on the horizon of the political changes which populist measures were to intervene quite brutally into regarding the role of art, education and culture in Dutch society, the Chto delat? group created one of its films, *Songspiel: The Netherlands 20XX*[66] at the Van Abbemuseum in Eindhoven. The film is a continuation of a series of similar works created by the Chto delat? in recent years and named *Songspiel*[67], with a clear reference to the works of Bertolt Brecht and Kurt Weill. The films feature dialogues set to music and refer to concrete social and political themes. For example, in the format of a short ancient tragedy, *Perestroika Songspiel* (2008) deals with the political hopes and visions of the future of those involved in the democratic changes before Gorbachev[68]. *Tower Songspiel* (2010) employs the architectural layouts of the Okhta Centre and the Gazprom Tower in St. Petersburg; its libretto again uses texts from true events and sets them to music. The result is a play on current Russian political and social life.

In 2011, Chto delat? made another film, *The Netherlands 20XX*, at the invitation of the Van Abbemuseum curator, Charles Esche. In the film, we listen to and watch a sung drama about illegal refugees who find shelter in a museum in an indeterminate but hardly incredible future when the state is governed by strict laws about migrant deportation. The dramatic musical dialogues unfold between the museum guards (the representatives of the people), the museum director, the journalists, the authorities, an artist and the refugees, touching upon the problematic situation of a refugee family whose presence could endanger the artistic institution. In the film, an artist exhibiting at the museum proposes to give refuge to the family of migrants, by using its members in the reconstruction of the avant-garde opera *Victory over the Sun*[69]. The second half of the film indeed features the refugee family performing amongst cubist objects; the film ends after the successful presentation of the reconstruction, with a sung dialogue between the museum director and a female co-worker. They express their satisfaction with the performance, which once again showed the museum's political engagement, and walk proudly through the collection of political and visionary works of the historical avant-garde that the museum is famous for. Although the performance again confirms the museum's revolutionary spirit to the satisfaction of both, the refugees are arrested on the following day, which, according to the director, "actually concerns us no longer."

The plot unfolds through sung dialogues, which has an especially strong effect; its elevated choral note shows that the tragic, heroic and unbridgeable antagonistic relationships actually take place in our daily lives. The tragic story has a profane ending; this testifies to the fact that political and ethical issues are all too often drowned in the cynical 'realism' of contemporaneity or in what Chantal Mouffe terms *the moral register of the political*.[70] Art frequently functions within a moral checklist; its works are addressed to all kinds of political problems, warning, educating and pricking with moral feelings of guilt and sympathy; however, they cannot bear the weight of the antagonisms that are at the core of art and also profoundly concern the institutions within which artworks achieve visibility and 'permanence'. *Songspiel* is thus a deliberately selected form of narration, bringing into the open especially the universal powerlessness of both political and ethical activity in art and posing the question of rethinking and conceiving of a different future. It shows that art, even if intensely thought of as a field of possible changes, actually does not possess such political power; in order to preserve its autonomous position of changing and conceiving of the future, it actually remains in the safe haven of the 'progressive' institution. Interestingly, all the works in the *Songspiel* film series deal with the future; the part referring to the Dutch situation predicts a new, menacing future lurking on the horizon, one far from the political and democratic hopes of the earlier films. In other words, contemporary art is marked by the inability to think of the antagonisms present deeply in its own core; rather than participating actively in changing common life, it rather continuously recognises the symptoms of its own disintegration.

I wish to use this example to enable an insight into the production of sociality in art; over the last two decades, this production has become so intensive that we can actually talk about social abundance. These shifts come in a variety of forms and are mostly visible in the expansion of participatory art or communal artistic processes. To put it another way: in the previous chapter, I focused on the body and subjectivity; in this one, I am going to deal with the intensities and articulations of plurality – with the place of numerous bodies and voices in contemporary art. I am going to discuss them in connection with the social processes of contemporary capitalism. My aim is to show that the production of sociality signals that art is actually closely intertwined with the processes of the disappearance of the sociality and political articulations of the public. The contemporary political pressures of increasing populism in Europe, the rightist attacks upon art and culture, and the neoliberal revaluations of human creativity and potentialities seem to have sharpened these questions even further. They are connected with the entry of sociality into production or with the exploitation of sociality and human relationships for the generation of market value, which profoundly shatters the public space as a space of antagonistic thinking or a space of the distribution of the sensual (Rancière)[71]. This places into question the emancipatory role of art, which was often at the forefront as a demand in the art of the twentieth century.

3.2. Relational delusions

At the end of the 1990s, the discussions on the political were heavily influenced by *Relational Aesthetics*, a book by Nicolas Bourriaud detecting the production of sociality in contemporary art and describing aesthetic phenomena, especially in the visual art of the 1990s. It is important to note that the text is a curatorial intervention, nevertheless it does flirt with theoretical argumentation to a sufficient extent that the book was well received immediately after publication and also frequently served as a theoretical foundation for reflections on new forms of communal articulations in art, the activities of the spectator and the autonomous fragmentary nature of the spectator's perception.[72] Social change and collaboration, social relationships and articulations are at the core of 'relational aesthetics', the notion that has influenced numerous participatory and collaborative artistic projects of the last decade. This work describes artistic institutions as spaces of social relations or numerous non-material processes that, as a flow of feelings, communications and perceptions, shape the new reality of the artistic market. Relational aesthetics deals with the processes of transition, participation, collaboration and contracts, in which artistic works are not only considered as social events (since they always take place in relation to the spectator), but also as independent formers of sociality by means of researching and establishing relationships (personal, political, economic, sensual, intimate etc.). Collaboration is closely connected to social change and the critical use of adaptable work processes that govern daily life. "The possibility of a *relational* art (an art taking as its theoretical horizon the realm of human interactions and its social context, rather than the assertion of an independent and *private* symbolic space), points to a radical upheaval of the aesthetic, cultural and political goals introduced by modern art."[73] At this point, I would like to analyse Bourriaud's approach, especially because he connects relational aesthetics with the political project; in other words, he ascribes political orientation to artistic work due to the social relations contained in the definition. The question that merits special attention is the following: what does Bourriaud actually talk about when discussing the political project – what kind of politics does the political in art refer to?

In her critical approach to Bourriaud's work, Claire Bishop points out the problematic dimension of relational works, which should be open to interaction, inviting to the collaboration and dynamic involvements of those participating. According to Bishop, the problem is that the relations established in this kind of openness are never established in connection with questions on how these works are involved in sociality, what kind of communities are actually formed through them and what kind of social reality these communities have.[74] Bourriaud's book thus entails a defence of art, whose non-material processes could be close to the artistic articulations of the 1960s, in the sense that they would not just reflect relations and connections but produce them. In this sense, artistic work would be political due to the active inclusion of the spectator and leaving the passive ocular observation of the artistic work that de-objectivises the work and dematerialises its processes. In this, Bishop warns of an interesting trait of the second half of the twentieth century; according to her, every work referring to participation already contains this rhetorical idea on emancipation as if activity itself were *a priori* connected to the political articulations of the democratic and the equality of subjects.[75] The question is how to evaluate and compare the quality of these relations, in which 'relational aesthetics' is never placed into question.

"When Bourriaud argues that 'encounters are more important than the individuals who compose them,' I sense that this question is (for him) unnecessary; all relations that permit 'dialogue' are automatically assumed to be democratic and therefore good. But what does 'democracy' really mean in this context? If relational art produces human relations, then the next logical question to ask is what types of relations are being produced, for whom, and why?"[76] According to Bishop, this kind of connection of relational art with the political project enables the direct correlation of aesthetic judgement with the ethical political judgement that is at work today in speech on the political character of art.[77] In this equality, the conclusion is somewhat like this: if relations are at the core of new forms of art, then this means that relational work (with all its traits such as the dematerialisation of the artwork as an object, instability, fragmentariness, openness, processuality, communal manners of articulation), are also political in the sense that they challenge traditional ways of understanding art and also change its perception. In other words: every communal form of collaboration is already supposed to be political and connected with ethical issues of being together, referring, establishing communal atmospheres, sharing, exchange etc.

If we follow Bourriaud, this is the reason why the ethical-political moment is no longer articulated through the traditional manner of utopian agendas, but in an active and involved manner here and now. It has active power in the sense that the life of those involved as art is supposed to offer many pragmatic and concrete suggestions of social change and community formation, which are also closely connected to artistic proposals. According to Bourriaud, we can talk about the microutopias of the present in connection with these works: the world does not change, but the active participants learn how to settle the world better; it is therefore about changing through direct social and communal collaboration, through play as well as the relations and protocols that the participants establish between each other – with work, the artist and, last but not least, the artistic institution.[78] But the question is whether this shifting of attention to social relations already constitutes political change or whether it actually intervenes into the communal ways of being together and the sociality of people. Numerous artworks that belong under the notion of relational aesthetics become works though the plurality of relations, i.e. through the changing multiplicity of numerous ways to be and be active (albeit temporarily) together. It is true that a more or less dynamic interaction can take place between subjectivities, but such an interaction never concerns involvement in opposing social relations; it never really questions the relations under which they are generated. Quite the opposite, such projects fuse with existing social relations and establish them as the only possible form. After all, this is also discussed by Bourriaud himself, who states that relational aesthetics reflects the shift from the production of goods (objects) to a service economy. It fuses with the shifts in late capitalism. Relationships are therefore a network of actions that bring the spectators, artists and curators closer together through the processes of the dematerialisation of objects themselves, but do not change the processes of spatialisation. They do not rearticulate either the space of the institution in which their meetings take place or the roles of those participating in the exchange of the relations in these meetings. The sociality created in this manner is therefore already framed and presupposed as the sociality of transparent artistic space, which, in a good neo-liberal manner, always verifies and improves the ways in which we refer to each other as social subjects, constantly offering new games for our subjectivities and producing political procedures of negotiation, agreement or disagreement, but actually with no real effect upon the antagonist space of the public.

Relational art should also not be equated with political projects because, in this case, spaces of art indeed become spaces of sociality, but this does not mean that we are already talking about public spaces. At this point, we can aid ourselves with Henri Lefebvre's understanding of space. Lefebvre develops the concept of active spatialisation, replacing the static understanding of space, and thus shows the importance of the role of space in the understanding of relationships and their "politicalness".[79] Space is not defined by the activity it is intended for (e.g. the tennis court, where tennis is played), or by the names of buildings and other firm identities. Space is always formed by means of active processes of spatialisation that result from the activities, physical traits and structures of subjectivities with their social relations, fears, desires etc. In this sense, contemporary artistic institutions (e.g. the museum or the gallery) are also no longer defined merely by the fact that they exhibit artworks, but are formed by the activities and relations of the social subjectivities that they are more or less temporarily settled by; contemporary institutions are open and transparent structures. However, these spaces are still those of separation and delimitation; actually, they are a lot closer to the negotiating and protocol spaces of contemporary democratic processes. Are not contemporary galleries and museums, as relational and communal scenes, similar to what takes place in the *antechambre*, a famous case of Lefevbre? Historically, the *antechambre* denoted the space for negotiations between the king and his petitioners, where the petitioners acquired more power because they met the king personally, with the monarch's power reduced by a degree for a moment because common subjects were close to him. It is therefore the most relational of all spaces; the mere act of entry into it changes the social position of the individuals, with them settling the space in a better way. Relational space is created because of the intertwinement of the relationship between space and subjectivity.

Lefevbre namely shows that the space of negotiations is not relational by itself, but can only take on this role when it is strictly physically codified as static and unchangeable. The most open and transparent democratic activity – that of institutional sociality – requires a strictly codified and unchangeable space. Negotiations can therefore only take place in a stable space that determines the procedure of the common in advance. A stable space still needs to exist in order to enable instability, the flow of dissent, the constant changing of roles and common activity. This is why it is not unusual that spaces for negotiation, collaboration and political discussion still remain among the most monumental and 'unchangeable' (parliaments, corporate buildings), and have also been joined by art spaces in recent decades.

The first conclusion to draw on this basis is that the institutions of art that open their doors to relational art have not really changed much, but have been entered by new atmospheres and tensions that constantly create the illusion of activity, co-decision and influence, which is closely connected to the pseudoactivity of the contemporary subject. Such pseudoactivity is connected with a constant flow of opinions and activities, as well as the forming of communities, but in such a way that the constant flow of relations is never threatened by incontrollable or unpredictable social dissent because these activities still take place in stable institutions with meticulously structured spaces. The second conclusion is that spaces of art have become spaces of sociality, negotiation and the seeming arrangement of social relations because such activity has actually disappeared from public space. On the one hand, artistic institutions take on the new role of the political space of negotiation and community creation, but frequently only in the sense that the stability of their spaces (closely connected to the capitalist economy and the production of value) minimalizes or eradicates dissension (as is e.g. clear from the work *Songspiel: The Netherlands 20XX*). An important part of these changes is the illusion of the social transparency of artistic spaces that constantly invite collaboration, multiple goings-on in various spaces, discussions, eating and temporary lodging in these spaces. New spaces of art must be entirely and constantly visible – they must create the possibility of participation and free activity. Lefebvre warns about this illusion of transparency. The space seems bright and clear, offering a free hand for activity; this is an illusion of a neutral and innocent space without traps. It is therefore important to conclude that here, it is not so much about the critique of relational art as such, but especially about a critical approach to its direct connection with the political. This connection only seems political because it entails and works with social relations. Today, these social relations are at the core of generating value, with manners of production connected to the exploitation of these relations. At the same time, the dematerialisation of objects and the fetishisation of open procedures and transparent relations are at the core of post-Fordist shifts in the understanding of work and production.

3.3. The Working Spectator

The production of sociality can also be analysed from another perspective – through the participation and active role of the audience at contemporary artistic events. Today, it is not just the artist who is social; the contemporary spectator needs to be as well. This mostly concerns events that take place at museums and other artistic institutions in large numbers; many of them are also located in-between the performing arts, performance art and visual practices. Due to the similarity of the production by means of human potentiality and energies, as well as due to the similar intensities, atmospheres and tensions between capitalist consumption and the consumption of art, I would like to point out a particular aspect of these events that can also be interpreted from the perspective of post-Fordism and modes of production of subjectivity. This chapter therefore focuses on the reflection on the participation and 'activation' of the audience at artistic events and the various performative actions that have been multiplying with great speed at art galleries and museum exhibitions in recent years. Events seem to be flourishing in the field of visual arts, hand in hand with the changing role of the audience. In various ways, the audience experiences the shift from passive observing or contemplation to activation and participation.

I would like to approach this discussion from quite a specific viewpoint and focus on the effort invested by the audience when it forms a constituent part of the artistic event. I would like to show that the 'effort' of the audience becomes an essential part of the contemporary artistic event. As shown by Rancière in his essay on the emancipated spectator, every audience is active; there is no difference in quality between "passive contemplation" and "active participation".[80] There are differences, however, in terms of the ways in which the event is constituted by the cognitive, energetic, physical, or emphatic strains of the audience. One of the main characteristics of contemporary artistic events is the central role of the 'effort' of the audience, which can also be connected to more general modes of contemporary work, especially with the ways in which the production of subjectivity is at the core of the economic production of today, as discussed in the first chapter.

In 2009, I was present at an artistic event that could serve as a nice introductory example for this chapter. For the closing party of the *In-Transit* festival in Berlin, the *artist* invited about a hundred people from the street to join her, promising them free food and drink under the condition that they started to dance and entertain themselves immediately, as well as actively inviting all the other participants to join in the party. It was the fastest outburst of dance I had ever seen at any party, although things did seem a little phony. The event was not actually constituted by the people hired to dance; the gist was not in them revealing the performativity of such social occasion. It was a lot more interesting to observe how fast the hired dancers actually succeeded in evoking similar social behaviour in the other party attendees. As a result, lots of people almost immediately yielded to the common joy and rhythm and immersed themselves in dancing until the late morning hours. What actually transformed this dance into an event was the social and affective work of the audience, its surrender, joy, going with the flow, its flirting with the rhythm and with other dancers, and its participation. The event was triggered by the change the audience created with its effort and investment. The event did not arise from the fact that this dance was provoked, activated and performed by 'temporary actors', but from the fact that it was shared, communicated, exchanged and danced together – that it gave rise to temporary alliances and energy flows in terms of joyful investment or active repulsion (depending on the decision to go or not to go with the flow). In this sense, it is the audience that is placed at the forefront in the contemporary event. In other words, the work is performed by an active audience; without audience participation, it would not be completed.

For this reason, it is sensible to think about that what it is that lies at core of the contemporary event; it is the social, affective and linguistic effort of the audience. I'm using the word effort intentionally because I would not only like to discuss a specific kind of effort, but also the exchange of power that opens the door for the audience into a temporary public space; its effort produces the added value of the event. At the same time, the audience works with its social, cognitive and emotional skills, i.e. skills central to contemporary forms of post-Fordist production. There is an exchange of work between the audience and the museum (or any other cultural institution where artistic events are performed); by means of its effort (affection, communication, emotions, desires, efforts connected with dispersion, organization, collaboration, isolation, etc.), the audience performs the work and performs the public of the contemporary museum. In turn, the museum enables and produces a platform for the public by means of letting the audience to do their work. In this sense, the artist stands somewhere in-between as a researcher of society and a cognitive experimenter, with the artist's work increasingly curated by the artistic institution so that it can belong to 'a specific public'.

If we claim that the audience's role in contemporary artistic events is actually in the effort, that there is a visible strain to a lesser or greater degree invested in the event, we need to ask ourselves whether it is also about a new form of exploitation. This question especially becomes intriguing because the audience of contemporary artistic institutions is no longer organized through the dispositif of watching (the passive observation of individuals); at the same time, it is also not recognizable as just an organized community of people or as a representational totality of a recognised identity. The audience of the contemporary artistic institution is embodied and shaped through endless rearranging, renumbering and various assemblages that can appear and disappear together with the negotiations, paths created or decisions taken by the audience at the exhibition. Contemporary artistic institutions soon seem like spaces where social experience is dispersed, incalculable and non-representative. The audience seems like a disorganized sum of fleeting and impermanent gestures, alliances, attractions, repulsions, agreements and disagreements – a sort of sum of fleeting glimpses of works and fragmentary thoughts. The contemporary museum does not organize the gaze, but rather disperses its effect. This is also why the contemporary exhibition often functions as a cacophonic space with a lot of delegation, interpassivity and going with the flow (which, incidentally, is also connected with exhaustion).

Quite frequently, the role of the contemporary artistic event is that of capturing the life force of such a multitude and performing it as 'the public', in the fact that the audience provides the event with a political, social and affective dimension. In this event, the indecisive multitude and its diffused effort transform into a public (social or even political) force. This is also why most artistic events, even the most immaterial ones (e.g. works by Tino Sehgal), actually do have a firm basis; events are namely based on the materiality of the effort and human force. At the core of the aesthetic arrangement of events, there is always human potentiality – that of the human gesture or the experience of life. Such an experience of life is truly social; even if it is diffused, fleeting or uncertain, it comes across as the performative nature of the variety of social gestures enabled by the artist's offer and carried out by the audience in the museum space. These experiences can of course differ as to the quantity of effort invested; they can be more or less powerful, more or less present, sometimes nearly unnoticeable and subtle, and at other times violent and deviant. Nevertheless, their exhibition value is always the same: they are at the core of the event and constitute the museum public.

In her introduction to the 29th Biennial of Graphic Arts catalogue, Beti Žerovc stresses the fact that numerous museums of today not only distribute and curate such events, but also take on the role of their producers and organizers.[81] I would like to add in this context, that, by doing so, the museums and other artistic institutions do not replace the traditional forms of sponsorship and commissioning of artistic works, but actually transform them into new production forces. Everything they touch they transform, not only into culture, but also into the appearance of the social. Everything produced at the museum seems 'public' by itself; the museum thus offers a performative shield for testing various social, affective and cognitive potentials of contemporary life.

According to Hito Steyerl, the contemporary museum "corresponds to the dispersed space of a social factory."[82] The museum is still a space for production, a space for exploitation; in the "museum as a factory" things are still produced. What continues to be produced are the forms of the social, created by means of an affective and communicative effort of the audience – by means of its senses, bodies and cognitive abilities, or, as Steyerl writes, the "aesthetic faculties and imaginary practices of its viewers".[83] At these new factories, exploitation continues to take place; it is present in the ways in which museums are productively organized: "as flagship stores of Cultural Industries, staffed by eager interns who work for free."[84] But this productive-oriented organization is not only related to the institution, but also to the ways in which it performs its public – the public that works and acts with its own social behaviour and social relations. In that sense, the role of the proliferating artistic events in the museums of today lie in the transformation of the art institutions into specific production places, factories of a different type. Paraphrasing the title of the first movie ever made (*Workers Leaving the Lumière Factory*) by Auguste and Louis Lumière, 1895), Hito Steyerl writes along these lines that workers actually never exit the factory. It is also no coincidence that many venues intended for contemporary artistic events actually inhabit former Fordist factories that were deserted after the relocation of Fordist production to non-Western countries. Occasionally, this invisible and brutally exploited workforce returns to the museum, to the now cultured and entirely re-designed Fordist factory in order to perform (as in Santiago Sierra's work with illegal immigrants, for example in *250 cm Line Tattooed on Six Paid People* from 1999). At such events, when the ones doing the work are people *sans papiers* – illegal workers, refugees or underprivileged people, whose existence is very often reduced to bare life – sociality is evoked through the audience's responsibility and repulsion toward these contemporary art events. Their ambivalent position is further stressed by the fact that they are temporarily paid by the museum institution in order to evoke a response from the audience and establish the 'critical public'. The old productive force returns to the museum as a Fordist ghost, creating a sense of guilt in the midst of social enjoyment at the new venues for the production of culture. But very rarely does this return of the workers actually create an antagonism that would endanger the institution itself and mess with the production of the public. This naturally puts a question mark over the institution, addressing the aesthetic spectrality of the production of political subjectivity.

The focus of artistic events has therefore moved from the autonomy of the performer or gesture to the autonomy of the audience, whose number, along with its strain (decisions made, behaviour, gestures and movements, presence or absence), establishes the work; these people actually work for the artwork. In this sense, Bourriaud is precise in his observation of the "relational aspect of contemporary works", where artworks are not only understood as moments of sociability but also produce the social through the exploration of relations.[85] However, there is something to this production of the social that is overlooked in his analysis. It concerns the essence of the problem of the political. What Bourriaud fails to stress is the question of exploitation: the social effort invested to create the audience of the museum, to create the new dispersed and autonomous public for the contemporary institution. This social is therefore not *a priori* emancipatory (or political in Bourriaud's sense), but part of the exploitation, going hand in hand with other processes of human exploitation in this post-Fordist mode of working.

The social thus produced is precarious, fleeting and affective, and it does not have a belonging, enduring, material or local character. This is the relational social that constantly improves, rehearses and develops the ways in which our affective and linguistic behaviours can be shared, negotiated, played and violated. This is also in accord with the shifts in the understanding of the museum's role in relation to the public – where the public is rethought as a multitude: "We do look at art, inhabit the spaces of art in various forms of collectivity, and in the process we produce new forms of mutuality, of relations between viewers and spaces rather than between viewers and objects. Beyond the shared categories of class, or taste or political or sexual orientations, another form of 'WE' is produced."[86] Rogoff writes about the performativity of relations, about the performative function of observation and participation, which forms an important part of the museum's public. Although this observation discloses the shift of the museum to more collective forms and rightly addresses the performative dimension of the audience, this statement is also problematic if linked to the heavy increase in such events. This 'we' of the contemporary public can namely be related to the invisible work that the audience performs at today's museums and by means of which it gives back the live and spectacular value to the museum as a place of active, common, political and rebellious contemporary experience.

Despite the live nature of the experience, the collaborative participation of the visitor and the dynamic character of the exchange, this is neither an authentic experience (which is more often considered the 'traditional' act of static looking) nor a personal one. Instead, and above all, it is a social experience of an event that must be endlessly circulated and shared. For this reason, the experience at a contemporary artistic event must be random, temporary and non-binding while the visitor often experiences their experience and shares it with others without any sense of belonging or responsibility. In recent years, artistic institutions have become places of sociality and community processes, laboratories realizing coexistence in various ways. But it is questionable whether this shift of sociality and community formation in the sphere of contemporary art really opens up possibilities for emancipatory political articulation, or whether this shift finds in the contemporary art institution a museum refuge for the vanishing processes and possibilities of life. In this sense, the exploitation in the scope of contemporary artistic events is very similar to the more general and all-embracing processes of subjectivization and the formation of communities in contemporary capitalism: it springs from the appropriation of human potentiality, human linguistic skills and affective forces.

The evidence supporting this claim can be found in the

various types of work performed by the audience at this type of event; they are very close to affective and cognitive work in general. For example, a short-term effort on the part of the audience, an effort that hardly represents strain, is frequently at the core of contemporary artistic events. On the other hand, there is plenty of social violence – a sort of rehearsal of delinquency, transgressions, aversion and negotiation. It is not usually about crude violence, but is usually mental, verbal and emotional, demanding from the audience certain skills, the acceptance of challenges, presence or absence, engagement or disinterest, which calls for many entirely different affective skills. Another skill that is frequently performed at these events is the exchange and circulation of gifts and obligations, again demanding from the audience work with affective powers and engagement in terms of 'critical' social situations. Such strains are very close to what is today frequently called affective and cognitive work, in which people work with their human potentials. Close parallels can be observed between the linguistic, affective and cognitive work of the audience at contemporary artistic events and the contemporary role of the museum as the disseminator and organiser of these forms of perception, which also reminds us of the problematic nature of several aspects of the contemporary production of subjectivity. In this sense, the people from the audience at the contemporary artistic event work as autonomous workers, managing their 'affective, social and cognitive skills'[87] in the scope of post-Fordist production.

It is true that contemporary artistic events are connected to the strong desire of numerous artists to emancipate sociality from production, establish another public sphere, engage in political gestures and rehearse disobedience. This desire gets caught up in the dispersed social space of the museum, where deviance from the capitalist system is systematically developed; however, the testing situation rarely transgresses the limits of the experiment. In that sense, "the museum is not a public sphere, but rather places its consistent lack on display."[88] According to Paolo Virno, this lack is characterized as the need for another public sphere – one where the creation of subjectivity would be tightly linked to creative, political and imaginative independence from the interests of capitalist production. At contemporary artistic events, we participate in the circulation of experience, which is situational, abstracted and ephemeral – an experience where lasting political or affective alliances are seldom formed. Actually, we perform the public (which capitalizes and consumes human and communicative forces) at the core of the lack of the public. This circulation of experience forms a multitude of visitors that has the "ability to anticipate unexpected opportunities and coincidences, to seize chances that present themselves, to move with the world."[89] This last quote is actually a description of the post-Fordist worker, but it can easily be used for the description of contemporary audiences at artistic events.

Contemporary artistic events can therefore also be understood as a kind of aesthetic and social training, playing at and experiencing forms of sociality – a sociality without continuity, a relation without belonging. "These are the skills people don't learn in the workplace; nowadays workers learn such required abilities by living in big cities, by seeking out aesthetic experiences, having social relationships, creating networks: all things that workers learn specifically outside the workplace, in real life in the contemporary big city."[90] In this sense, the museum factory as a dispersed social space produces a specific public sphere without the public, a constant training and exchange of linguistic, social and political activity but without the antagonism of an enduring location and without antagonistic consequences springing from social effort. In this, the artist is a facilitator, the one who creates the conditions to communicate and share. This also entails giving away the artist's autonomy to the audience in order for the artist to be exploited. Contemporary artistic events and performances have become exercises in social profanity and the exploitation of social forms: exercises in the pure profanity of the fact that our social activity no longer has a public dimension. In this sense, the museum is a social factory that the workers have returned to, or, as Steyerl would say, never really left.

The first movie ever made, *Workers Leaving the Lumière Factory*, shows the movement of workers leaving through the factory gate, with the place of work left in darkness. Now, the workers are returning to the factory and the place is becoming increasingly illuminated and social; the work is shown (performed) more and more. It is illuminated through the display of a lack: what it truly lacks is an outside, another public sphere that would use all these social skills and strains to form a new political subjectivity.

To conclude: in the last decade, especially with the transformation of artistic institutions into 'places for sociality', the contemporary art institution very often has the role of capturing the life force of such a mass and performing it as the 'public'; in this, the audience is provided with political, social and affective dimensions. At the event, this unidentified mass and its dispersed effort are transformed into a public (social or even political) force, and the abilities of the audience are on display. It would not be enough to conclude that contemporary artistic institutions just appropriate the 'life force' of these performances and freeze the experience into spectacle. Such a statement would imply that the participatory events of several decades ago were somehow more authentic than their contemporary reanimations. Something else takes place in the exploitation of audience ability.

In many contemporary works focussing on the social, affective and cognitive abilities of the audience, there are unfounded parallels drawn between the activation of the audience and 'the public', where the participants with their social abilities and potentiality to act, perform an inseparable community between the audience and the public. Rancière discusses the problematic aspect of the theatrical reforms in which the difference between the two places (the stage and the place of the audience) is abolished in order to achieve an inseparable community. He strongly defends the difference between the redistribution of the spaces as an intellectual adventure on the one hand and, on the other, rejects the demand that the theatre as a venue should achieve the gathering of an inseparable community and become an indispensable common place. He compares this wish to the platonic assignment of the bodies to their good, common place.[91] I would like to point out that his findings can also be used to disclose the dynamics of contemporary performative and participatory events in visual art (especially in the light of its renewed interest in performance over the last decade), where the problematic is the same.

The activation of the audience and the display of its abilities blur the dividing line between the audience and the artistic work, in which a common experience of art is presupposed (e.g. in theatre reforms). At the core of this common experience is a shared democratic dispersion of actions or free assemblage of individual choices. This tells us how strongly this shift to the activation of the audience is connected to the belief that the contemporary experience of art is democratic and that it can be understood as an enumeration and equal dissemination of possibilities, decisions, choices or deviations. Interestingly though, this experience of work can only be shared if the artwork itself actually disappears, if the artistic event is reduced to the sheer display of problematic sociality, which cannot really be judged (indeed, by what criteria could the gesture of sociality be judged?); it is continuously disseminated, accumulated and shared as a immaterial experience of social relations and abilities. Such an accumulation of social experience transforms the artistic institution into a peculiar common place, with the activation of human capabilities at the core of the aesthetic event. For this reason, it also directly reflects the cultural and economic traits of contemporary production: the accumulation of immense social production or the production of sociality is the main drive behind today's economic values.

"We learn and teach, we act and know as spectators who link what they see with what they have seen and told, done and dreamt. There is no privileged medium as there is no privileged starting point. There are starting points and knot points everywhere from which we learn something new, if we dismiss firstly the presupposition of the distance, secondly the distribution of the roles, thirdly the borders between the territories."[92] In this sense, the audience is always active. It needs to be considered that every spectator is already an agent (in their own story etc.). This activity of the spectator is always negotiated in connection with a third condition: the emancipation does not take place due to the erasure of the distance between the two parties (the artist and the audience, the stage and the audience, the artistic venue and the audience), but due to the intermediation of a third condition, an in-betweenness, which is actually the artwork itself. The intermediation of the third condition is key when we discuss intellectual emancipation and the ways it can be connected to the participating role of the audience. This intermediate condition is the artwork, assessed from an unpredictable and unbridgeable distance.

Due to the problematic blurring of the dividing line between the audience and the work and the equalling of the audience with the public, an erasure of the ability to judge takes place, which also enables the transformation of our social abilities into the unity of spectacle. The whole negotiation process is only possible due to the intermediation of a third party (artwork, book, poem, the artist's subjectivity, especially in performance art). The process was aptly described by John Cage in connection with his work 4.33: "The performance should make clear to the listener that the hearing of the piece is his own action – that the music, so to speak, is his, rather than composer's."[93] This is a description of artwork, which we know only exists as a radical denial of its means, but at the same time also discloses the main common condition for the separation: the work that persists between the audience and the author. The listening ability is therefore not about a social gesture, but about a constructive and active aesthetic component of the work itself, which is a result of the negotiation between numerous separations and arrangements of abilities. In this sense, we wrongly equate participation with the desire to be with others and share our abilities for what is common in the work. We also falsely equate the audience with the public instead of always viewing it as separate from the public, as something by means of which we temporarily leave the public outside and rehearse new adventures in how to be together through being separated.

3.4. Between One and Many: Collaboration

In the first part of this chapter I mostly discussed the ways in which sociality enters art and how the excess of sociality changes the role of the spectators or the public to which the artistic work refers. I focussed especially on visual art, where a marked shift towards more participatory and performative forms of artistic work can be felt; this shift must be examined together with some traits of contemporary capitalism, changes in the status of contemporary visual institutions and changes in the way in which participatory work is understood. In this part of the chapter I would like to show that these changes in the way of working also affect the contemporary performing arts.

I am not going to focus on the relation to the spectator; the spectator is already at the centre of discussions on the performing arts due to the nature of the medium. It is more interesting to reflect from the perspective of the excess of sociality; this enables us to see new processes of work in the performing arts in relation to the omnipresent production of sociality in capitalism.

In a newspaper column, the philosopher Renata Salecl once described the story of Randy Pausch, which also raises numerous questions in connection with the symptomatic relationship between time management and collaboration.[94] In 2007, Carnegie Mellon University organised a series of lectures entitled *The Last Lecture*, for which professors were asked to talk about what was really on their minds. If they had to deliver the last lecture of their lives, what would that have been like and on what subject? The invitation from the university with the rhetorical implications of determinacy was clearly intended to challenge the lecturers and prompt their imagination to yield some added value. The challenge got an entirely different twist to it in September 2007 with the lecture entitled *Really Achieving Your Childhood Dreams*, given by Randy Pausch, a Carnegie Mellon University professor of computer science. After stating that he had been diagnosed with terminal pancreatic cancer and only had half a year left to live, he began to talk in an optimistic and humorous way about his childhood dreams, giving insights into computer science and also giving advice on creating multi-disciplinary collaborations, group work and interactions with others. All this was accompanied by enchanting life lessons and even push-ups on stage. His lecture immediately received media attention. The lecture video became an online hit on social networking sites such as YouTube, Google Video, etc., and within a few days, the promise of Rausch publishing a book of his lecture was worth between 6 and 7 million dollars. His story was followed by the inevitable spectacle, with compassion growing parallel to market value.

I begin the chapter on collaboration with this story because there are several coincidences involved that can disclose the amazing relations between the experience of time and collaboration. A surplus of the story that merits our attention came about later, when professor Pausch, at that point a celebrity, was already fighting the terminal stage of his illness. Surrounded by the media frenzy in which collective identification was growing parallel with the anticipated profit from his works, Pausch agreed to give another lecture at Columbia University, in which he discussed time management. He talked about the most efficient ways of making use of time, how to create manageable plans, multiple schedules and efficient meetings, and how to go to bed with an empty inbox. This was something Pausch was an expert on in his life, but it of course acquired a completely different, much more metaphysical dimension when he accepted the aforementioned invitation. Salecl describes the obsession with time management as a desperate attempt to look behind the unbearable mask of death. There is no mystery behind the final fact of death or – whatever our strategy may be – behind the obsessive time management or refusal of all timelines; all strategies are equally unproductive.[95] The last period of Pausch's life is intriguingly commemorated by the book *The Last Lecture*, which, apart from providing optimistic life guidelines, also deals with the subject of collaboration and ways of collaboration in research and time management. The strange combination of issues together with the unavoidable life prognosis is neither a result of a publishing strategy nor purely coincidental. It can also be understood as a peculiar symptom that discloses the strange relationship between time and working together, a relationship that is inescapable nowadays: in contemporary society, working together cannot be conceived of separately from time management.

I would like to argue that today there are important economic, political and philosophical reasons for the fact that collaboration is understood as a time-bound constellation demanding perfected time management, organisation and division. From the perspective of the contemporary political economy, the work processes of collaboration are inseparably connected to time planning. In this, contemporary capital is not only considered something by means of which time can be measured in very concrete terms, but also as progress: in the political economy, there is also an element of innovation in time. In other words, we layered and parallel experiences of contemporary time, which must be carefully planned regardless of the possibility of openness and liberation, and have a special, effective time structure. Their chaotic and multi-layered experience needs to be rationalised by means of operative and effective procedures, in which subjective experiences are necessarily subjected to the common goal.

This argument is also supported by an important work maxim of the last few decades: that of working together. As Florian Schneider writes, teamwork has been a key notion in the transformed political and economic climate of the 90s; as a synonym, the word cooperation is often used. Based on an understanding of the management theory that people are supposed to understand and believe that thinking, planning, decisions and actions are better when taking place in collaboration with others, teamwork serves as a key notion for success, in accordance with the famous maxim of Andrew Carnegie from the early twentieth century: "Teamwork is the ability to work together toward a common vision, the ability to direct individual accomplishments toward organizational objectives. It is the fuel that allows common people to attain uncommon results."[97] As Schneider further writes, teamwork also represents the subjugation of workers "to an omnipresent and individualized control regime. The concept of the group has replaced the classic one of 'foremanship' as the disciplining force. Rather than through repression, cost efficiency was increased by means of peer-pressure and the collective identification of relatively small groups of multi-skilled co-workers."[98]

For this reason, teamwork is part of the obsessive administration of the neoliberal subject, who has to be free from their inner constraints – creative, innovative and virtuous. The subject, who, at least since the late 1960s onwards, has been able to reveal their subconscious desires and free themselves from the permanent feeling of mortality. At the same time, this creative all constantly behave as though we were in an already decide race (in which numerous deadlines need to be met), in which i is the abstract goal that determines the present of the process, it temporal dynamics as well as the ways in which this process is to be articulated, carried out and measured. In this sense, it is even easier to understand the collective identification with the determinacy of the lifetime we still have left: it springs from the sudden and entirely desperate impossibility of relationships – from the horrible experience of the desperate inability to administer our lives.

"What then is time? If no one asks me, I know what it is. If I wish to explain it to him who asks, I do not know." (St. Augustine: XI, 14) In this statement, St. Augustine links the difficulty of articulation with the ontological understanding of time. In his theological thought, time is strongly connected to the mystery of the divine. Approaching the statement from the contemporary perspective, we can find that, today, this unpronounceable ontological understanding has been replaced with a guidable and explicable notion of time. This means that the contemporary experience of time entails a knowledge of what time is. This experience of time can also be connected with the frequency of the statement 'Sorry, I don't have time'; this, of course, is yet another description of our general time experience. The contemporary acceleration of time, a consequence of the industrial, economic and scientific processes of the last two centuries, not only disperse the spatial coordinates of worl processes (their fixed and static territoriality), but have als changed the manners of individualisation of contemporar subjects. According to Jameson, contemporary temporality schizophrenic in nature. It is about the temporality of t present, but without any kind of phenomenological connectio that would enable us to cling to the past or foresee the futur However, the experience of the contemporary subject and individuation of the human being are achievable through m and value-generating subject is free from the restrains of society and the difficulties posed by differences and otherness. Not only can he/she freely work with others, otherness itself becomes a value in collaboration. In this obsessive administration of the subject's self, refusal is only allowed occasionally; from time to time, it is possible to escape, maybe on holiday, into drugs or (most unfortunately) to hospital. The paradox is also that the immaterial work force, into which so much hope for collaboration has been invested over the last few decades, is (as Matteo Pasquinelli ironically stated), in a kind of "immaterial civil war" and not a struggle against new forms of exploitation: "It is the well-known rivalry within academia and the art world, the economy of references, the deadline race, the competition for festivals, the envy and suspicion among activists. Cooperation is structurally difficult among creative workers, where a prestige economy operates the same way as in any star system (not to mention political philosophers!), and where new ideas have to confront each other, often involving their creators in a fight."[99] Can we then imagine a different mode of collaboration that would not inevitably end in having no time at all, precisely at the point when we actually begin to collaborate? Can we also collaborate with no revolutionary, corporate, metaphysical deadlines on the horizon? As Schneider argues, the question is how new dimensions of working together could be reflected on, conceived of and at the same time distanced from the "free wheeling and well-meaning strategies of anti-authoritarianism on the one side or the brutal force of coercing cooperation on the other".[100] What is it, then, that makes collaboration transformative and how do collaborative subjects really inflict change?

Today, it is so difficult to think about collaboration as a transformative process because there is a certain excess of collaboration in our daily lives: we become most visible when collaborating. Not surprisingly, collaboration is a key issue, not only in politics (which is somehow cynical given the other meaning of 'collaboration', which is connected with treason), but also in contemporary economy and culture. Collaboration is closely related to the mobility and flexibility of contemporary labour and even seems to be inscribed into the value of labour as based on the constant production and exchange of communications, relationships, signs and languages. Collaboration locates people in the present (time); it is only through collaboration, on the constantly changing map of places, that people can actually become visible in the present, where they constantly add to the contemporary flow of money, capital and signs. Interestingly, the other can most frequently be encountered in the same working community that enables this contemporary mobility: more and more 'non-collaborative or non-belonging' people or groups move in the invisible and deadly channels of illegality, poverty, invisibility and flight. We could say that collaboration, communication and connection belong in the most fetishized fields of the present day. According to Paolo Virno, the fundamental abilities of the human being are currently at the forefront of production, with language, thought, self-reflection and the ability to learn as the principal characteristics of contemporary public labour. Contemporary production consists of common linguistic and cognitive habits (i.e. the affective and intellectual exchange of knowledge); it is the constitutive element of the post-Fordist production of labour. "All the workers enter into the production as much as they are speaking-thinking. This has nothing to do, mind you, with 'professionality' or with the ancient concepts of 'skill' or 'craftsmanship': to speak/to think are generic habits of the human animal, the opposite of any sort of specialisation."[101]

For Virno, this can be denoted as preliminary sharing, which is the basis of contemporary production. In his view, sharing is in opposition to the traditional division of labour. There are no longer objective technical criteria to regulate working together and to define the responsibility of each worker in their own specialised sphere. Or, as Virno writes, "the segmentation of criteria is instead of that, explicitly arbitrary, reversible, changeable."[102] Along these lines, the interesting notion of the process of sharing can also be interpreted as a specific understanding of collaboration as an exchange of differences, creations and innovations and no longer as the hierarchical division of tasks. For Virno, the problem arises when such sharing has no political effect and does not effect change within a political community. "The public character of the intellect, when it does not take place in a public sphere, translates into the unchecked proliferation of hierarchies, as groundless as they are thriving."[103] This influences the ruthless mode of individuation in terms of the complete subjugation of the worker's self or, in Virno's words, results in "personal dependence", which I already discussed in the previous chapter. The fetishized status of collaboration can also tell us something about what Virno terms the "non-public public sphere", which reflects the one-dimensional character of the global networks and communication channels. "Because this sphere is not a political sphere, the non-public public sphere thus created can produce the most devastating consequences: collective hallucinations of fear, occult forms of superstition and general paranoia."[104] Or, if we apply this to the notion of collaboration: when collaboration fails to inflict change within the public sphere, it is not part of *res publica* and can produce unrestrained forms of oppression.

It seems that there is something about our daily rhythm, in the way we experience this sharing of language and thought, which pushes us into a state of constant mobility, flexibility and precariousness, where nothing is stable but the deadline of working together, and where space is generated as a consequence of mobility.

In 2006, Eleanor Bauer, an American choreographer and dancer based in Brussels, completed her research on the Brussels dance community. In her text, she humorously tackles the notion of the mobility of contemporary performance artists, the changed status of this flexible and disembodied labour, and the value of the community that has resulted from such collaborative mobility of artists. Besides offering picturesque descriptions of the mobility of the contemporary performance artist, with an obligatory Mac computer and multiple toothbrushes, one of the last paragraphs of her research describes the performing artist in the following way: "The performing artist him/herself is a resource, a located node of activity and hub for information that processes and produces within the interstices of culture and community. In a neo-collective or post-collective model, the artists that remain in pro-community engagement must maintain a highly individual-oriented strength and productivity while remaining connected to the world and to each other, each highly differentiated while in constant collaboration with a larger network of other creative, productive individuals that support and engage in each other's interests. This description is ambitious considering what it requires in terms of time and energy, and generosity of course, as we are not paid for keeping in touch even when our work depends on it."[105]

Let us ask ourselves, where this accurate description of the highly ambitious performance artist actually comes from. Is this not the description of the contemporary worker, equipped for continuous high performance? That of the always critical and active labourer, whose subjectivity is entirely subjected to the modes of contemporary capitalist production? The fact that the performance artist has some generosity and even collaborates free of charge doesn't save him or her from the contemporary forms of exploitation. The generosity puts him/her at the core of the contemporary mode of individuation, where it is precisely their extra time and energy that are demanded from the subject. Couldn't that description also be read as a description of an artist who desperately struggles with the public character of their work which, at the same time, is not public at all (except maybe within a small, specialised operative circle of people who delegate value to each other)?

Over the last decade, collaboration has become a key issue in the vocabulary of dancers, choreographers and other performing artists. There are many performances dealing with collaboration as well as conferences and lectures on that subject. As Myriam Van Imschoot writes in one of her letters on collaboration in contemporary dance, the word appears very often, "it gained a currency of a catch phrase." However, "do we speak more about collaboration because dance makers collaborate more than they used to, say, a decade ago?"[106] The interest in collaboration could, of course, also be connected with the changes in the understanding of artistic subjectivity. The subjectivity of the artist is no longer understood as a singular, self-centred subjectivity. The process of artistic creation is now much more oriented towards the research-related, transdisciplinary and performative aspects of work. This can also be related to the disappearance of professional divisions, as discussed by André Lepecki. For some time now, the divisions between choreographers, dancers, critics, producers and dramaturges have been fading. Thus, each of these professions has theoretical and practical knowledge from other fields at its disposal – another factor that reinforces collaboration and makes it visible in contemporary artistic policies. Lepecki relates this disappearance to the dissolving of the stable epistemological categories of "what dance is", which has also caused changes in the position of the artist, critic and producer.[107] Such changes have resulted in different models of collaborative work and become part of the contemporary cultural policies and economies of production. As Imschoot writes, this reorientation on the artistic scene may explain why the collaboration label circulates more frequently, but "it does not explain why it does so with so much emphasis, to the point of sheer over-determination and a compulsive repetition of the term. It seems as if collaboration functions as uncritical marker or signifier, an honorific that must signal more than it actually performs."[108] The notion itself is linked to a certain crisis; the high frequency of its use reveals that there is some sort of anxiety at work in the use of this term. I would agree with Van Imschoot that there is something highly problematic at work in the compulsive repetition of this term. This repetitive use is tightly linked to the changed notion of labour, where language and the thinking being are at the forefront of contemporary production. The anxiety springs from the inability to really inflict change, to make the processes of collaboration part of *res publica*, to open up one's political and transformative potentiality. What Imschoot detects in this obsessive use and practice of collaboration is that, ultimately, we have no time at all. What takes place is an anxiety of subjugation, an unbearable attempt to look behind the mask of the race determined in advance, whereby, at the same time, we just won't admit that we are already participating intensely in that same race.

It is well-known that, from the second half of the twentieth century onwards, we witnessed a lot of research on the nature of artistic collaborative processes. When analysing those processes in the visual arts, the art historian Charles Green showed that those processes sprang from a particular crisis of the singular artistic subject; they were a result of the crisis of authorship as such. The outcome of those collaborative processes was not necessarily more democratic and didn't result in a more dispersed working process. As Green noticed, authorship was reinforced in most cases; collaboration therefore gave extra value to the contemporary artist's self.[109] The visibility of collaboration processes is therefore tightly linked to the development of cultural production and economic processes in contemporary culture. As I wrote earlier on, this visibility was further reinforced by the language and creativity coming to the forefront of contemporary production. With new communicative possibilities, collaborations became multiple and simultaneous: "People meet and work together under circumstances where their efficiency, performance and labour power cannot be singled out and individually measured; everyone's work points to someone else's. Making and maintaining connections seems more important than trying to capture and store ideas. One's own production is very peculiar yet it is generated and often multiplied in networks composed of countless distinct dependencies and constituted by the power to affect and be affected. At no point in the process can this be arrested and ascertained, for it gains its power by not having explicit points of entry or exit as a normative work scenario might."[110]

Schneider points out the power of exchange and sharing, but these can only be purposeful and unimpeded if they enter the public sphere, which is connected to the notion of possessing knowledge, storing ideas, copyright and the right to contemporaneity. Artists of today collaborate, but they can be prevented from doing so if their collaboration becomes yet another capture machine for the privatisation and storage of ideas. As a partial exception, let me mention the artistic collaboration that is developed under the influence of open code and other ways of programming and sharing within the community. Among the choreographic projects, let me mention the Everybodys Toolbox platform; based on the open code model, which is intended for sharing choreographic procedures, working methods, assignments and rules (scores).[111] In this way, numerous methods of working have opened up to the sharing of artistic processes under the influence of open ways of working and thus have productively broached the hierarchical problem of authorship. Nevertheless, we must not forget that today parallel network manners of working have been replaced by blogs and social media. In their scope, collaboration frequently represents yet another way of exploiting our communicative work. With our investments and constant communicative work, we actually participate 'free of charge' in the capitalisation and privatisation of electronic networks.[112]

Today, things come to a halt due to an excess of collaboration, which makes the artist 'contemporary' in the sense that the artist belongs to the present, but his/her position as such is not radically changed; there is no potentiality to this halt, only actuality.

Nevertheless, the excess of collaboration could also be read as a particular reminder, one that is also discussed in Imschoot's letter. She explicitly writes that the notion of collaboration might also be a cover-up for its antidote, "genuine exchange."[113] What is genuine exchange though? Can we talk about a difference between collaboration as a procedure (for its own sake) and true collaboration? The problem is that such a caesura springs from the remedial but naïve hope that there is always something more real than the relationships in which we are already continuously participating. This is a complex problem and can also become a kind of trap that leads to nostalgic, utopian longing for proper encounters, which have disappeared. At the same time, this problem of 'genuine exchange' is extremely challenging. I could relate it to a statement by Badiou that Slavoj Žižek cites at the end of his book *Violence*: "It is better to do nothing than to contribute to the invention of formal ways of rendering visible that which Empire already recognises as existent".[114] In this book, Žižek analyses the problem of violence and discusses it in connection with the harsh critique of participation and constant demand for political activity. After several examples, Žižek ends the book by refusing any kind of action; paradoxically, this stance comes at the end of the book, when the book has already been written.[115] The demand for a refusal of action comes at the end of some very agile activity. This should not be understood as a paradox but as something that reinforces the power of critical analysis. It discovers the possibility of the potentiality of critical articulation, which was active due to the urgency of the refusal.

The demand for 'genuine exchange' can thus be a reminder, a trigger that can help us talk about the potential of collaboration as an agent of change. We need to think about the future of collaboration in the rupture between an impossible refusal of the collaborative process in which we are already implemented, and the possibility of genuine exchange, which has yet to happen. The future is not related to actuality as a realisation of its 'becoming', but finds itself in the rupture of something which has yet to happen. In this sense, the imaginative potential of collaboration can open to the wide and unpredictable practice of working together. But in order to enable this, we have to deal with the excess of collaboration, with the fact that the reflection on collaboration takes place at the moment of its crisis. This crisis deeply affects the way we think about the future of collaboration and the way we relate it to potentiality.

"The absolutely desperate current state of affairs fills me with hope".[116] Marx's remark not only discloses the idea that the antidote is quite close, but also a special relation to time and historicity, which, according to Leland Delandurantaye, can also be found in Benjamin's and Agamben's work.[117] Benjamin describes the vision of the drowning man, and Agamben develops the concept of radical potentiality, which discloses the critical reversibility of the moment, i.e. the present time itself. Giorgio Agamben writes about the inevitable paradox of this peculiar philosophical concept of potentiality. You can only become aware of your potential to exist, create and take a step forward when this potential is not realised. Therefore, potentiality is a temporal constellation, separate from action; it is not translated into action at all. Potentiality can only come to light when not being actualised – when the potential of a person or a thing is not realised. An intrinsic part of potentiality is a certain failure, an impossibility of actualisation. Only when the potential is not actualised is one open to one's being in time. . In this openness, one experiences *the plurality of the ways* in which life comes into being and is exposed to the plurality of possible actions.[118] Today's crisis springs from a permanent and ruthless actualisation of potentiality; in this, the form of temporality itself (the manner in which a human being becomes human) is entirely conditioned by its finalisation. The actualisation of potential has become a primary force of the value on the contemporary cultural, artistic and economic markets. To put it another way: with the rise of new ways of working (non-material work, affective work, cognitive work), the primary capital sources of value became human language, imagination and creativity. This transition came about in many different ways and it can be seen quite clearly, for example, in the constant re-questioning of the conditions that produce new states of production. The present time of permanent actualisation also profoundly changes the ways in which we perceive and experience collaboration. The problem is that, due to this kind of exploitation of human potentiality, collaboration has been structured as a specific time mode where collaboration equals actualisation, an obsession with the present time.

In the future of collaboration, it would be essential to intervene into its aforementioned excess and radically rethink the exclusivity of the present – the thing that brings people together into common work. This is only possible if the collaboration takes place without the impediments of the present: the impediments caused by deadlines, speed, simultaneous connections, the illusion of mobility, the hypocrisy of the difference, the illusion of eternity, and constant actualisation. Today, it is quite difficult to preserve in potentiality (but perhaps nevertheless easier due to the major crisis that is on the horizon and has already refuted so many predictions), open the path towards the material conditioning of actions and foresee future events independently of the already given scenario. How can common work be open to unexpected change? It is time for us to return to the issue of time and its connections with collaboration in artistic processes or in the creation of performance. If collaboration represents common work, the decisive factor will be the quality of the meeting that enables this common work – the quality of time.[119]

3.5. A Portrayal of Non-Functioning Community

In addition to his visionary critique of spectacle society and his notorious drunkenness, Guy Debord was also known for his ruthless exclusion of even his closest friends and collaborators from the Situationist movement. The entire history of Situationism can be read as a series of exclusions and rejections of many notable members. This is also one of the main reasons for the regular renaming of the movement, which served to disassociate it from the former collaborators. Some of the popular ways for Debord to cut people off were to publicly refer to the inappropriateness of their characters and even publish their obituaries, as in the case of Wolman and Potlach in 1957: "Wolman had an important role in the organization of the Lettriste Left-wing in 1952, then in the foundation of LI. Author of 'megapneumic' poems, a theory of 'cinematochronicity' and a film, he was a Lettriste delegate at the congress of Alba in September 1956. He was 27 years old."[120]

Ironically, there is actually no better form of necrology for disclosing the main flow of time. The flow of time was significant to many collaborative artistic movements of the twentieth century, especially to the political and artistic avant-garde movements; aiming for future revolutionary goals as the supposed vanguards of history. The necrology for the excluded member of the movement is not a sign that the avant-garde and revolutionary flow of time is progressive and therefore ruthless to everyone who does not follow the timeline of the most vanguard community of collaborators. More interestingly, such a timeline is deeply ambivalent and causes splits in the abovementioned avant-garde artistic communities, which seem to be collectively 'tuned' to the society of the future. According to Susan Buck-Morrs, it is about a kind of schizophrenic temporality where the revolutionary time that still has to come exists parallel to the present, in which the latter needs to be more active than ever before (that is, if we do not want the future project or revolution to fail). Buck-Morrs writes about simultaneous temporality when analysing the time structure of the revolutionary state, which is always divided into the time of the revolution and the time of the regime.[121] This simultaneous time structure can also be implemented on a smaller scale – in the collaborative structure of the (artistic) community oriented towards finality: the future can only be the goal when the present is fully activated in its collaborative agency – alliances, collaborations, working together and being together. Nevertheless, there is a rub to all this, and this brings us to its schizophrenic character: the future is only possible if the present is sacrificed at the same time – when the social connections are continuously erased. There is a difference between the time that still has to come and the time of present events, defined by processes like friendships, alliances, love, working together, collaboration and being together. Communities focussing upon a common future goal are not based so much on the erasure of subjectivity in the collective sameness but on a certain spectralisation of even the closest other, in which the other is always already present as a ghost, no matter how strong its present agency is. Under the heavy burden of radical choice (a paradoxical choice, that is, since no choice is really possible), the friends' ghosts are thus caught in the ungraspable gap between the future and the present.

Twentieth century art history knows many collective achievements that, on the one hand, constantly publicly disclose their collaborators as expelled others and ghostly heretics in the name of common future goals and, on the other, constantly seek alliances and friendships on the basis of which the artistic production becomes reconfigured. Nevertheless, too many ghosts and failures have contributed to the fact that communities with collective ideals are ridiculed nowadays; there is a lot of disappointment in the idea of community in general. But is it nevertheless possible for the community to exist and not fall into such a double time structure where the other can only be nearby as a ghost?

Without a doubt, the communities of the 1960s were very different from the hierarchical organisation of the Situationists. In 1967, the actors and members of the Living Theatre group invited their audience to protest and join them in a common act of bodily and sexual liberation on stage. The famous performance entitled *Paradise Now* not only revealed the awakening of the ritualistic character of the art of the 1960s; it can also reveal a different concept of community and its collaborative structure. The performance was created in a period of huge political disappointments over both political and personal situations, when there was a strong need for the liberation and exploration of new ways of being together. One rebellious sentence from the performance precisely describes what was at the core of these explorations: "I'm not allowed to take my clothes off. I'm outside the gates of paradise."

As its title formulates with great precision, *Paradise Now* was a way to liberate personal, intimate and sexual desires. New communities can be built as those of equals, friends, brothers, sisters and lovers, who can all be together in the present time of sensation and pleasure, in the present of the aesthetic reorientation of perception and sensuality. That's also why the members of the audience were invited to join in on the spot and to explore and search together with the members of the theatre group for ways of liberation and also – very importantly – for ways to do art. Nobody was excluded in advance, everyone was welcome as capable of collaborating and making art. The communities of the 1960s are undoubtedly quite different from the spectral collectives of the avant-garde. One of the biggest differences can be found in the collaborative structure, which is no longer caught in the split of ambivalent time structure, but discloses the power of the present time in its endless agency. Or, as demanded by Alan

Kaprow in connection with the new art of happening: "all our senses have to be alert, only then can the artistic situations unfold themselves as naturally as the wind ruffles the tree leaves and something can transpire that is as ubiquitous as walking down a street."[122] For art to constantly hold on to the present, be constantly alert in its senses and disclose desires, the community somehow became much more embodied in its manner of collaboration. We can also say that the collaboration became bodily and fleshy in character. This is a different notion of community, where the bodies collaborate with each other, creating alliances of libidinal energies and basing the common being on desire. Due to the democratisation of the community, the collaborating other appeared as a body; examples of that would be the desiring bodies of *Paradise Now* or the bodies of Marina Abramović and Ulay, standing close together in *Breathing In/Breathing Out*. According to the convictions of the time, bodies placed close together were able to aesthetically reconfigure time and place, which would have enabled the freedom and liberation of every individual and intimate part of the community.

The collaborative structure of the communities in the 1960s is therefore very different from the collaboration of ghosts, caught in the gap of history under the heavy burden of radical choice. The flow of bodies and liberated senses can only take place if they are simultaneously present as differentiated particularities and individuals, only as differences between desires and investments. In this case, the collaboration happens under the light burden of endless choices, including the exploration of liberation in *Paradise Now*: "all creative actions form out of some kind of freedom, nothing bearable happens without some kind of freedom". The collaborating other is present through an immediate freedom of choices; this freedom of choices provides it with his/her body, senses, particular desires and creative energies. There is also a strange paradox at work here; very interestingly, it can be observed in the practice of contact improvisation, which first emerged in the early 1970s. The movement is developed through the freedom of the body to improvise and choose depending on contact with the body moving close to it. Why is it, then, that the ultimate performance is more or less the same every single time? The endless participatory freedom of bodily collaborators, the spontaneity of the democratic communities from that period, is only possible through a series of strict protocols that enable a 'free' collaboration scenario because they are merely technical. Participatory freedom is thus always the freedom of realization through a certain protocol that allows us to participate and do whatever we desire without hindrances. As is well-known today, forms of power were not eradicated in the 1960s, but underwent a fundamental change; the power inhabited the networks, modes of collaboration, the protocols of the private, the flows of the corporeal, the microstructures of intimacy. The paradox at the core of participatory freedom is that every form of participatory freedom requires the same scenario for the body to be free. This becomes problematic when the closest other is the body: bodies only participate and are free within the already given scenarios for different others, inside the already given scenarios for 'free' desires. Today, this paradox of the 1960s communities is at the core of the contemporary production of desire, where the scenarios for freedom are increasingly unified, privatized and controlled. Consequently, the other is also increasingly represented and produced under previously given scenarios: 'paradise now' is a world of prêt-a-porter identities, bodily styles, glorified differences in the desiring unity of the present time.

People tend to work with each other, they want to be together and share work together; what is it that holds them together? The French philosopher Jean-Luc Nancy offers a way to bring back the corrupted notion of community by changing the notion of community as finality to the ordinary state of being together. "Community on the contrary is the ordinary being together, without any assumption of common identity, without any strong intensity, but exposed to banality, to the 'common' of existence."[123] It is therefore not a depiction of the common as dominated by finality that can take different forms (total man, society without classes, the liberated body, liberated subjectivity, etc.). The common is also not something that is tightly intertwined with the active transformation of twentieth century history. Instead it is merely the ordinary state of being together, deprived of all historical tasks. "The retreat opens and continues to keep open, this strange being-the-one-with-the-other to which we are exposed."[124]

This new understanding of community is also evident in some other artistic work by Chto delat?, the group I started with and would also like to conclude this chapter on the production of sociality, particularly because it is about a group of artists and theorists who are closely connected to the topics of working and collaboration, but in an entirely different way to their predecessors.

The sociality of collaboration is also at the core of their early video work *The Builders* (2005), which I first saw exhibited in a dark room on two projection screens hanging next to each other.[125] One constantly displayed a slide-show of photographs of the Chto delat? members, and the other the English subtitles to their informal conversation in russian coming from the speakers. The photographs showed a group of informally clad young people with drinks and cigarettes, standing next to and sitting on a weedy wall on a rather cold night. The people talk and change postures, hug, lean toward one another, touch, support one another, turn, sit or stand, push each other back and forth or smile to each other. Their discussion takes place on a single spot as if they were shut into a painting.

They are actually connected with one – their video namely starts and ends with *Builders of Bratsk* (1960), a famous portrait by Viktor Popkov. It shows five workers (four men and one woman) resting in their collective creation of the new city of Bratsk. Embodying all the qualities of the socialist-realist style, this famous work served as an introduction to the Chto delat? video display, in which its members start and end their discussion in exactly the same poses as those of the workers portrayed. It is therefore about a display of work relationships that seems the same, but also could not be more different. "Our group meets quite rarely and this piece was the result of one of those rare meetings. Actually, we've been wanting to make a piece about our community for quite some time, to tell about who we are and what are we doing. A kind of self-analysis, in other words. What inspired us was Viktor Popkov's marvellous painting *The Builders of Bratsk*. This is why we called it Builders. But we didn't try to imitate the heroes of this painting. For us, the feeling that we're building something is important, so we tried to find out what exactly are we building..."[126] This is the beginning of the filmed discussion, followed by a fragmented dialogue on "what is community", how people can work together and reflections on what lies in-between art and capitalism, politics and theory, on the role of exchange and conflict, on how to bring about changes in art and create revolutionary art, on communism and community, the status of artists and activists after the fall of communism and the end of social utopias etc.

The staging of Viktor Popkov's workers can also be read as a sort of historical trace of removal, leaving only the frame, the disposition and the staging, a phantomic disposition of bodies. Or, as one of the voices in the video comments on the portrait: "I can derive some aesthetic pleasure from this painting, but it doesn't move me socially." The frame in which the bodies are similarly repositioned also establishes the connection and emphasizes the difference between both groups: that of the builders of Bratsk and that of the Chto delat? builders – the artists, writers and activists who would also like to build something, bring about social change and actively reflect on social and political revolution. It seems that this kind of thinking can only take place if we also consider the ruins of the shattered communist ideals and the major disappointment hanging over all the possible constructions of society. Their choice of frame leads to the conclusion that community and common work cannot be discussed without also establishing an attitude with what has not yet been done. Although starting their discussion in the same positions as those of the workers from Bratsk, they seem to be together accidentally and placed incoherently into an anonymous space. The question that is in the air and that will remain in the air throughout this chapter, is difficult because of its simplicity: how can working together be possible amid the ruins of community?

The work by the Chto delat? group could of course also be discussed from the perspective of the specific political and social conditions in Russia, in which the political and activist status of artists is especially threatened due to radical political ideas and new ways of working. The victorious political forces of the last decades that have established themselves on the ruins of communist history are erasing any memory of the articulation of alternative social and political desires, especially those articulated in connection with the common.

The questions that arise from the conversation of the Chto delat? members and their accidental common being can be connected to the broader interests in terms of community and collaboration that have been strongly present in the field of visual arts and contemporary performance over the last two decades. The disappointment with the sense of community and the shattered utopian political ideals is, let's say, mutual, with numerous artistic works starting to reflect on the community and common work and reformulating them.[127] The work by the Chto delat? group therefore displays two different ways of being together and two different articulations of the community. If a community is understood as a description of a group that has something in common, the people in Viktor Popkov's portrait are together because of the common future they are creating with their brigade work. It is this community that is at the centre of this portrait; the workers' positioning in space is also intended as an ornament, a representation of the order of the community. There is an interesting surplus to this group of workers building a new city: the group is portrayed at their moment of rest – one of the men is smoking while the two men standing with the woman are doing nothing at all, just looking ahead. Their seemingly working bodies are light and relaxed as if on a short break; perhaps they are observing the growing city, looking ahead at the future that is still to come. In this future, there is naturally no difference between work and free time; this interesting surplus actually reveals the totality of the society of the working men and women who, in their moment of break, are staring at what they are jointly creating.

Directed ahead, their gaze can also be interpreted as a look into an entirely known future; we face the portrayal of the common as a finality, as a known society still to come; they were portrayed at the moment of building it. According to Jean-Luc Nancy, this finality can take various forms (total man, society without classes, liberated subjectivity etc.).[128] The other display features a group of young people changing places, opposing one another, joking, bickering, discussing, but the sequence of their photographs is more reminiscent of those rather common social nights with cigarettes and booze than of a position of work. The difference between the two displays is in the manner in which the common is portrayed.

In Popkov's portrait, the common is the only thing portrayed. The people are together because of their common future: community is at the centre of the portrait, which allows for no additions whatsoever. This common embraces the people during both their work and rest. When this image is replaced by that of Chto delat?, we are suddenly overcome by the feeling of coincidence, that they accidentally happen to be together in the presence of the night without a representation of the common and without a portrayal of order. The young artists are not together because their common being would be subjected to progress, teleology, finality or a future common goal. Along Nancy's lines, this would then be the 'common' of what is termed 'always already' – what we share in connection with banality and daily life (the issue of one's own finality, for example), the 'sacred profane', which positions us in the picture in an incoherent fashion. This is a community without exchange, universality, economy, coherence or identity for there is nothing that could be shared; there is no common being. In other words: community consists of the retreat of the common. A community has therefore little to do with a future common goal or with being unselfish, sharing things, taking responsibility for one's actions and respecting another. It also has nothing to do with the consensus for collaboration and the pluralist procedures of democratic dissemination. It is not about the outcome of dividing the property we share and dividing it in a democratic and proportional manner.

What, then, is community? Paradoxically, it is the constant dispossession of collaboration and its possibilities. Community can only be arranged; according to Maria Galindo, "we place ourselves next to one another, back to back, one in front of the other, according to the necessities of each specific struggle". The words of the Bolivian artist, feminist and activist disclose some important (dis)appearances of the collaborative other from the perspective of the present: "We can only speak in the first person. We are neither interpreters nor spokeswomen of each other's practices and actions. We do not speak in the name of one another because I am 'the other' when I express what I believe in and feel, within a scenario that was never given or borrowed." This performative gesture of autonomy helps us avoid constantly talking for the other as well as being constantly talked about ourselves. The need to speak in the first person has little to do with the freedom of choice to speak for ourselves, or better still: with the possibility to embody our special selves in the already given scenario of freedom. Galindo states this quite clearly: "I am 'the other' when I express what I believe in and feel."[129] When speaking, she already discloses "this strange being-the-one-with-the-other to which we are exposed"[130] discussed by Lean-Luc Nancy in his description of the community of the usual common being. An incessant articulation of space and time occurs. By means of special language, Galindo explicitly shows the appearance of the common: the moment we speak in an explicit manner, we become the other and the connection between meaning, space and time becomes visible.

When reflecting on the community and understanding of collaboration in the Chto delat? member exchange, another interpretation becomes significant. It discloses the moment of collaboration as part of immaterial work, as work with communicative and human potentialities and no longer as a representation of the totality of work. In this sense, the communities are much more coincidental and flexible and are not connected to a certain space; they are actually not united by work, but over the very specific temporal dimension of meeting.

A meeting is something that enables or prevents life; this is the purpose of meetings, both in life and thinking, Agamben writes.[131] Collaboration conditions our future life together; if we wish to unclasp time, this naturally means that time needs to be taken out of the obsession with the future and collaborate in the time that has not yet come. Common work is a temporal constellation that opens up the spatial potentiality for closeness, something that comes across as a neighbouring space, a space added.

Agamben describes an example of such a constellation, which he calls "ease". According to him, ease is a semantic constellation where spatial closeness always boarders the appropriate time: if the time is not appropriate, the topos that enables the meeting does not exist.[132] This means that a 'genuine exchange' has something to do with potentiality – with the ways in which we condition our common future. We could not work in the direction of the future without simultaneously changing our way of life, the material protocols of life itself, the way we shift time and experience it. To collaborate means to belong to another temporal concept – potentiality. This is the temporal concept of "time's darkness, the hushed shadows massing about the stage of what happens".[133]

Chapter 4
Movement, Duration and Post-Fordism

4.1. The Free Time of Dance

In this chapter, let us once more return to the film *Workers Leaving the Factory* (1895). It shows workers from the Lumière factory as they flow through the factory door, leaving their workplace at the end of the day. The same film also opened the performance *1 poor and one 0* (2008) by BADCo., a Zagreb-based performance group.[134] The mass exodus from the factory not only marks the beginning of cinema history, but also the problematic connection between the cinema and work, which is also explored in Harun Farocki's documentary and text with the same title – *Arbeiter Verlassen die Fabrik* (1995).[135] In his commentary on the documentary, Farocki states that the primary aim of that movie was to represent motion using the mass exodus of the workers. In Farocki's opinion, there may even have been signs used to coordinate the movement of the workers. Interestingly, this invisible moment takes place along specific lines, those marking the difference between work and leisure time – between the industrial process and the factory on the one hand and the private lives of the workers on the other. The movement of the workers, their simultaneously organised and spontaneous dispersion in different directions, is choreographically organised and filmically framed along the line separating enclosed industrial space and private life, strictly rationalised life procedures and so-called flexible leisure time. This is a line between dull work organisation and leisure time when the workers can enjoy themselves; in other words, it divides the mass organisation of work and the atomised private lives of the workers. The dispersion of the workers renders their workspace invisible: the door of the factory is closed after their departure and the space of work is left in darkness. Farocki mentions that throughout cinema history, the inside of the factory has only been illuminated when somebody wants to leave, demolish the factory or organise a strike. The inside of the factory has therefore only been featured when it becomes a space of conflict rather than a dull and repetitive space of work routine.[136]

The entire performance *1 poor and one 0* revolves around that dividing line by means of constant re-entering through the aforementioned door, marked with a simple crossbar on the set. The performers repeatedly come through that door, copying the movement of the workers in the Lumière factory movie. It almost seems as though they were in a motion picture experiment by Edward Muybridge, combining many short sequences of movement to give the impression of time coordination. In-between those scenes, they discuss work-related issues: "What happens when you get tired? What happens when you leave the work behind? When the work we devote ourselves to makes us too exhausted? What comes after work – is it more work? What happens when there is no more work?" These discussions in the performance make clear references to the historical aspects of twentieth century work, especially to the gradual disappearance of that dividing line. In that sense, they add another aspect to Farocki's observation. The place of work is no longer in darkness, but dispersed everywhere; it is not only a constituent part of leisure time, but intrinsically connected to creative and transformative potentials. Through the constant repetition of movement from the 'the first choreographed film ever', the performance becomes a collection of fragments and memories of movement, revealing that the first movie arrives through a door that now seems to have been taken off its hinges. The movement of the workers gets captured on a doorstep that no longer exists; today, there is no longer a dividing line between the body movement subjected to the rational organisation of work and the dispersed atomisation of society. Not only is the division between work and life erased in post-industrial society; the once essential qualities of life after work (imagination, autonomy, sociality, communication) actually turn out to be at the core of contemporary work.

How is the disappearance of the dividing line between labour and leisure time related to contemporary dance and the conceptualisation of movement? To be able to answer that question, I would first like to briefly reflect on the appearance of twentieth century contemporary dance forms, especially on the fact that their aesthetic and political potential was continuously formed in the complicated relationship with existing production modes. There are many intersections between the organisation of work production and the conceptualisation of movement in the history of contemporary dance (Taylorism, movement reforms, the return to the natural body, etc.); these intersections become especially intriguing when they intertwine with the political and aesthetic potential of dance.

It is well-known that, from the beginning of the twentieth century, new dance forms were experienced as something strongly connected to the potentialities of the contemporary human being. The autonomous movement of the body opened up new potentials of human experience and relationships, and had strong emancipating effects on understanding the future. The new, modern forms of dance (Isadora Duncan, Martha Graham, Mary Wigman etc.) seemed like a break-up with the old perception modes, whilst showing the possibility of new aesthetic experience. This was because of the intrinsic relationship between movement and freedom, which was presupposed in almost every attempt at movement reform. As Bojana Cvejić states, even today, "dance still works as a metaphor for going beyond contracts, systems and structures as models of theorizing subjectivity, art, society and politics."[137] According to Cvejić, that may be the case because "movement operates from the middle of things. Makes us step outside the pre-determination of points and positions. Expresses the potential of moving relations."[138] It therefore seems that movement is intrinsically political, in the sense that it tackles the interrelations and dynamism of expressions, the potentiality of what movement could or could not be.[139]

In that 'middle of things', movement also operates within the introductory image from the text, in the image where we see the workers exiting the factory. The movement is captured on film only to disappear into an unknown future; nevertheless, it starts at a particular doorstep, which frames the potential of moving relations in a very specific way. This potential is developed outside the rationalised organisation of work; it is the potential of movement that springs from life without work. The alliances, relations and divisions exist outside the factory, in the space without work, which not only becomes a political space, but also a field of autonomous aesthetic experience where the crisis of the subject and new forms of kinaesthetic perception were developed and institutionalized through the history of art in the twentieth century.

It is therefore no coincidence that the dance reforms of the early twentieth century appeared at a time when the movement of the working body in the Fordist factory was heavily rationalised – i.e. when the organisation of production was based on the scientifically researched kinaesthetic experience which instrumentalised the movement of the body for efficient production. The (mostly female) pioneers of dance (Isadora Duncan, Loie Fuller, Ruth St. Denis, Mary Wigman, Valentine du Saint Point etc.) started dancing at a time when the organisational model of work became omnipresent, when any kind of false, expressive, slow, stationary, unexpected, wrong, clumsy, personal, lazy, ineffective, imaginative, additional movement was eliminated from the work performed by the body.

The utopian relationship between movement and freedom in the beginnings of contemporary dance and dance reforms were therefore not connected to the notion of abstract freedom, but expressed the potential of moving relations outside the factory door. This was a freedom of different kinaesthetic experience, which would not yield to instrumentalisation and efficiency and would not be subjected to work but discovered the inner potential of the body. One of the ways of describing this experience is the discovery of the 'natural body', which does not have so much to do with resistance to the mechanisation of contemporary life (whereby the term 'natural' could wrongly imply that it is only about the division between the natural and the artificial), but with the discovery of a new universality, a natural sympathy of one body for another, which is also described by John Martin for example.[140] The moving relations are no longer subject to dull routine and rationalisation, but vibrate part of the new atomised society of capitalism; they are the relations between the new kinaesthetic subjects.

I would like to argue that the appearance of dance reforms and modern dance provided a moving alternative to the kinaesthetic experience behind the factory door; subject to strict rationalisation and efficiency, which experience was completely different to the free relations between free time subjects. Movement experiments were also an important part of Fordist production and the social distribution of bodies in the industrial phase of capitalism. Scientific management (Taylorist) theories, for example, focused on the perfect synchronisation of the body with the machine, which demanded a radical and absolute interiorisation of movement in the body. Only in that way could the gestures of the body be separated from the experience and endlessly repeated; we could say that the working gesture can be separated from the experience of work.

The bodies of industrial workers are usually described as machines and their automatic work as alienated. Lurking behind such alienation is an interiorisation of movement so radical that the body of the worker actually becomes alien to the one who works with it. Only when the movement is radically interiorized can the body become alien – the other body, which can serve the state or the factory. We are not dealing with the alienation of movement from the body, but with the radical interiorisation of movement in the body, so that the body becomes a space of constant quantitative division upon minimal and highly effective moves. Only in that way can a spectral and efficient working gesture be created and the movement not experienced as a change.

For this reason, Fordist production was often represented as synchronous group dance moving together; this dance often functioned as a critical representation of the subjugation of the worker's body to the industrialised and mechanistic factory production process. It does not come as a surprise that many popular representations of the assembly line introduced a clumsy worker who interrupted the group work process with his unforeseeable gestures, like Charlie Chaplin in *Modern Times*. These mocking and incapable workers destroyed the entire production process because they were too dreamy to be efficient and too clumsy to work well. This also means that they experienced movement as change. Rather than being efficient, they demolished the rationalised rules of movement. Rather than moving smoothly, they reacted to the obstacles and the materiality of the machine, with their uncontrolled gestures springing from their relation outside the body: they were being moved by the world and the objects they operated. The only way to disturb this collective process was often by means of the intervention of an individual body, a body that couldn't follow or was too clumsy, slow, dreamy, lazy or expressive – a body that took too much freedom to move, express itself or achieve something. The bodily traits that prevented the body dancing together with others were considered expressions of humanism, or even better – that of uncontrollable human nature, which cannot be disciplined. The individual kinaesthetic experience strongly resisted the group harmonization and its subjugation to the rationalised social machine.

However, there is a difference between the interiorisation of movement in dance and the Fordist approach to movement; ultimately, workers can hardly dance, they have to work. Scientific management was therefore successful in interiorizing movement. It also tried to abolish any kind of additional pleasure that could expose the phantasmagorical character of the institution and thus expose it to ridicule: pleasure was radically expelled from the body. For this reason, modern dance pioneers at the beginning of the twentieth century re-evaluated the dynamic between the outside and inside of the body. They searched for a different kind of pleasure, connected to the autonomous aesthetic language of the body, which frees itself from the institutional and disciplinary grip. We can even say that the feeling of modernity and contemporaneity of dance, this disclosure of the kinaesthetic potentiality of the body, was connected to the new kinaesthetic experience of leisure time, to this unknown and dynamic transversal outside work, which is no longer subjected to the rational organisation and instrumentalisation of movement.

This is where we come to the core of the freedom implied in the emancipatory potential of dance. In the conceptualisation of movement in dance reforms, this was the freedom of time without work, the discovery of the potentiality of leisure time as opposed to the dull routine of movement at work. Movement expresses the potential of the moving relations in the creative time of the non-working subject. This can also be linked with the emerging consumer class, where movement opens to the unexpected, imagination, privacy, chance and flexibility, disclosing its expressive power. In this case, leisure time also becomes a time for new aesthetic experiences. Contemporary dance had to develop new techniques that would transform this freedom into a language, develop the open virtuosity of the moving body rather than the instrumentalised product, and open up spontaneous movement as aesthetic language rather than the scientific naturalisation of movement. In this sense, the political and aesthetic potentiality of twentieth century dance was strongly intertwined with the exit from the factory.

What represented an expression of freedom in the capitalist societies of the twentieth century was considered a sabotage of society in a different ideological constellation – a representation of obsolete individualism, unable to adapt to the new transformations of society. I especially have communist countries in mind here, where the image of dancing together functions as a depiction of societies where the dividing line between the factory and private life was erased for ideological reasons. Communist systems adopted all the movement reforms in the production and work process, but with a different conceptualisation.

Socialist defenders of Taylorism (including Lenin himself) understood the scientific management of work as the management of the new society, where the door between the factory and private life would no longer exist. Beyond even this, there was a lot of discussion among Soviet communists and Russian avant-gardists about the hidden potentials of Taylorism and Fordism, which, in their opinion, went unnoticed by the Western capitalists who invented the two. Lenin writes that the Western (capitalist) implementation of Fordism resulted in the alienation of the workers and an authoritarian organisation of work. Socialist reformers and avant-gardists believed that the new modes of working together could transform society in general. The simultaneous movement of the workers was understood as a transgressive and transformative poetic form through which the development of a new society could be achieved. This was also the conviction of A.K. Gastev, one of the chief engineers and directors of the Central Institute of Labour in Moscow (he became director in 1920). Not only did Gastev introduce Taylorist methods in the USSR and develop them further, but was also a famous poet celebrating the new power of industrialised labour and the merging of the human being with the machine. In his poems, he developed a rhythmical language to describe new production, where the workers would move and transform the entire historical epoch by means of their joint labour.

"When the morning whistles resound over the workers' suburbs, it is not at all a summons to slavery. It is the song of the future. There was a time when we worked in poor shops and started our work at different hours of the morning. And now, at eight in the morning, the whistles sound for a million men. A million workers seize the hammers at the same moment.

Our first blows thunder in accord. What is it that the whistles sing? It is the morning hymn to unity."[141]

It is well-known that the movement reforms of the Russian avant-gardists (e.g. those of Meyerhold, Foregger, and partially – in another context – those of Laban) were heavily influenced by the new production process in terms of its abstraction and rationalisation. The aim of movement reforms was to develop an effective gestural language. In other words, they wanted to develop a new kinaesthetic dynamism that could be achieved by means of the efficient use of gesture and the instrumentalisation of the body. For example, Meyerhold began to rationalize the movement apparatus, in which the actor's body also became a model for a general optimization of movements. Although his work was closely connected to Gastev's and Taylor's utilitarian production models, Gerald Raunig states that the methods Meyerhold employed went in another direction: he also wanted to denaturalize theatre.[142] Contrary to the psychology of the plot, the empathetic audience and the singular kinaesthetic experience of the dancing body, which developed an autonomous aesthetic language in the West (especially in North America), the movement in the concepts of the Russian avant-gardists (or important components of biomechanics) consisted of the rhythm of language and the rhythm of physical movement – the postures and gestures arising from the collective rhythms that coordinated the movement of the body and that of the bodies with one another.

In the twentieth century, we can therefore observe two different relations between the conceptualisation of movement and the organisation of production (work itself). In the so-called western societies, more accurately described as 'capitalist', we can analyse processes of movement naturalisation that opposed the instrumental use of the working body and the rational organisation of society. This naturalisation of movement runs in parallel to the discovery of the singular subject, a desiring individual with his/her transversal and transgressive dynamic movement outside the modes of production (metaphorically speaking, outside the factory gates). This individual is mostly understood as constantly in movement and in a process of continuous creativity and autonomous aesthetic language, an individual who cannot but dance.[143] Another proposition came through the factory gate – the idea that the modes of production could be intertwined with the transformation of society in general.

The movement reforms of the historical avant-gardes erased the doorway between work and private life; they came across as kinaesthetic constructions of future worlds. In the movement reforms of the Russian avant-gardists and the European avant-garde (especially the Futurists), the fascination with industrialised production modes led to experiments in the denaturalisation of movement, where the body became a field of experimentation for a future social transformation and an understanding of future commonalities. In this, dance and the production process opened the way to the exploration of a new generality of the human being, a generality that comes before any kind of individualisation in the sense of the political generality of the future that is still to come.

Unfortunately, the discovery of the movement of this generality was an utter failure; it quickly lost its emancipatory political potential and became a totalitarian unity of the communist regime. In capitalist societies, clumsy, still, expressive, lazy, dreamy, everyday and marginal movement is understood as an intervention of liberated singularity; in communist societies such movement sabotages the whole social machine. In their utopian pursuance of the future, communist societies erased everything that radically existed in the present, cynically believing that the future had already arrived. It is therefore not surprising that the communist regimes actually celebrated the most conservative and disciplinary forms of dance, like massive gatherings of people or disciplinary ballet institutions.

The immense aesthetic and political differences in the early twentieth century must be connected with the processes of the radical interiorisation of movement at many different levels, including the approaches of contemporary dance pioneers. In spite of all the differences, the dance pioneers re-evaluated the dynamic between the inside and outside of the body, with the dance artists (mostly women) wanting to liberate movement and bodily expression as a force coming from the inside of the body. In these reforms, human subjectivity became the ultimate source of movement, a source so strong that it could abstract its own body into an autonomous aesthetic field. In this case, we are talking about the disclosure of inner freedom as a specific kinetic abstraction that can therefore also be connected to the fact that, in the conceptualisation of movement by dance reformers, this freedom was the freedom of time without work, i.e. the discovery of the potentiality of leisure time as opposed to the dull routine of work movement.[144] This comparison between two conceptualisations of movement, with the political potential of dance in the movement of the singularity on the one hand, and the discovery of the new (political) generality of the human being on the other (especially in the case of avant-garde conceptualisations), gives rise to a very interesting observation from today's perspective.

We are namely living in a time when the door between the factory and leisure is being erased, when the potentiality of the individual and autonomous creativity are at the centre of production. The movement of this working rhythm is very different to the description in Gastev's poem, which actually celebrates the disappearance of the factory door. Instead of the synchronised totality of work, which he extols as a new transformation of society and represents with the image of 'everybody starting at the same time', the new transformation of today's society takes place through disharmonious working rhythms, flexible work times and individualised and displaced work. The factory whistle is replaced by free-will and silent deadlines, driving people into many simultaneous and connected activities in life and work. Celebrated throughout the twentieth century as the discovery of the potentiality of freedom, the movement of the individual now stands at the centre of appropriation; its affective, linguistic and desiring aspects are exploited. We have to dance in a flawless and conceptual diachronicity while creating the present and changing places, times and identities; this must take place with speed and with only short (but not very destructive) outbursts of crisis. This is the new universality of the post-industrial world and its mode of production.

This brings us to *Pontoffel Pock, Where Are You?*[145], a 1979 cartoon by the well-known American cartoonist and satirical author Dr. Seuss (Theodor Seuss Geisel). Once again, we chance upon a satirical image of workers dancing together; the working process in a pickle factory is depicted as a harmonious musical. However, one of the new workers, Pontoffel Pock, is quite a loser – clumsy, disruptive, poor and unhappy. Clumsy by nature and a daydreamer by heart, he tries to push and pull the machine like the other workers; his eagerness to do well destroys the entire factory and he is accompanied to the exit in disgrace. In his self-pity, he is approached by an angel, who introduces himself as a representative of a global corporation with branches all over the world. As the corporate angel sings, Pontoffel Pocks life is to be pitied and he is offered a magic piano; he only needs to play a few tones and push the pedals to fly to any exotic destination in the world and experience the most beautiful and exciting adventures. He again causes trouble with his behaviour – due to his unpredictable gestures and movements, due to his desiring body and to 'always being in the wrong place'. He simply cannot enjoy himself and be spontaneous, but always breaks social relations with his ill-timed actions. This goes on until he finds the love of his life (an Arabian princess) and gets one more chance at the pickle factory.

The cartoon offers a good example of the shift that took place in the early 1970s and can today be described with the notions of post-industrialism or post-Fordism, especially in connection with the modes of working. The main characteristics of this shift are great changes in the organisation of production and the role of work, influencing social relations in general. Creative, linguistic and affective work becomes the centre of production. Work is no longer organised in an instrumental and rationalised manner, behind the factory door, but becomes part of the production of sociality and the relationships between people. Creative, spontaneous, expressive and inventive movement, which used to be excluded from the denaturalised movement of the Fordist machine, is now at the core of production. The essence of contemporary production calls for creative and potential individuals, with their constant movement and dynamism promising economic value. Illustrating production as a form of dancing together is obsolete nowadays, also due to the ineffectiveness of its social critique. Today's Fordist machinery moves away from visibility to countries with a cheap labour force with no escape to leisure, only a brutal exploitation of life in all its aspects. The contemporary post-Fordist worker is no longer part of the rationalised machine, but rather that of affective and flexible networks, with his or her potentiality up for sale.

However, there exist new forms of dancing together that are much more connected to the kinaesthetic arrangement of everyday life, which is closely connected to the ways in which we live and work today. In 2006, Natalie Bookchin created a video installation entitled *Mass Ornament*, in which she reflected on the role of mass ornament of today.[146] At the beginning of the twentieth century, the mass ornament functioned as an aesthetic reflex of the rationality of the prevailing economic system, which I analysed as a rationality that heavily interiorized movement so that the body could effectively produce. So, what could a mass ornament be today?

The question gave rise to the aforementioned work by Bookchin; she collected hundreds of YouTube videos of people dancing and made them into a synchronous choreography. Everybody dances alone in his or her own room, usually with a television screen in the background where the same dance is performed. Bookchin choreographed and composed the recordings on the basis of similar moves, gestures and dances that the dancers had made in private. The result is a peculiar choreographic distribution of bodies dancing the same dance or in the same way, always alone, in private yet nevertheless in a public and connected way. Such choreographic distribution could easily be achieved by means of a computer algorithm (if it had the right parameters like 'find people dancing to Shakira's song', or 'find people turning their heads in the living room' etc.). Such automatic selection and combination is actually performed regularly in surveillance centres where recordings of security cameras are analysed.

In comparison to the universal rationality of Fordist production, Bookchin's work creates an ornament of isolated private rooms and the showing-off of bodies exposed in their difference, which is also a difference of radical sameness: a movement where change is but spectral and replaced by a constant quantitative division of the differences of those who are trying to learn the same popular dances and show the same virtuosity.

This tells us that the exploitation of the human ability to move does not have the same ideological constellation today that it had in the disciplinary societies where movement was interiorized so deeply that the body became a kinetic machine, a small but smoothly operating cog in the giant social machine. The role of movement in post-Fordism has to be analysed in connection with the exploration of everyday movement and 'what bodies usually do', i.e. how they move with the world. This not only speeds up and erases the 'ontological slowness' and transformative potential of bodies, but creates a radical incongruity between the 'movable ones' and those expelled to eternal stillness.

If we claim that movement stands at the centre of production and that it is exploited as human potentiality, then this also implies that, today, change or alteration is radically abstracted from it. Movement only exists as an accelerated flexibility of contemporary subjectivity. In this way, movement enables freedom as temporal enslavement. We could say that, due to the appropriation of movement, "productive powers shade into powers of existence."[147] The non-materiality of contemporary work, its 'spatial' independence, is based on the exploitation, or even better, the exhaustion of these generic human forces – i.e. on the appropriation of movement as one of the forces of life.[148] This means that the production of today is experienced as something spontaneous and flexible, where the process of work is always subject to our own initiative.

In this sense, we can also understand another image of dancing together, one that has been appearing in recent years in the countries of the post-industrial world – the huge flash mobs organised by corporations and TV companies. On the surface, these dancers seem to celebrate the spontaneity and affectivity of human relations; what they really celebrate are commercialised joy and spectacular togetherness. It is therefore necessary to rethink the consequences of the changes in the modes of working for the conceptualisation of contemporary dance, especially if we claim that the political and aesthetic potentiality of dance was discovered in relation to the production process. What would the consequences for contemporary dance be with these changes in mind? What would the disappearance between work and non-work mean for the relation between dance and freedom, which was always kind of self-evident when reflecting on many dance reforms of the twentieth century?

First of all, it should not be overlooked that the relationship between dance and freedom no longer has anything to do with resistance to the rigid and disciplinary production modes. Unexpectedness, non-hierarchical structures, affectivity and linguistic/bodily expressiveness have entered post-industrial production and represent the core of post-Fordism as the new organisation of the production we live in. The autonomy of creativity and aesthetic experience, which was so important when the resistance to the rationalisation of labour first emerged, now represents an important source of production value. We therefore have to observe the relationships between contemporary dance and the new production modes, which have placed movement and constant flexibility at their centre, along with expressive and spontaneous individual creativity.

Today, subjugation consists of constant movement, flexible relations, signs, connections, gestures and a continuous dispersion outside the factory gate with the intention of producing (and spending) even more. The production of today encourages a constant transformation and crisis of the autonomous subject, with the intention of capturing that subject's creative outbursts and transmuting them into value. There has to be ceaseless collaboration, temporary but not too affective, otherwise it can become inappropriate and destructive.

In an interview, Paolo Virno describes the way post-Fordist workers acquire their skills. The qualities of a post-Fordist worker never require skill in the sense of professional expertise or technical requirements. Quite the contrary, what's required is the ability to anticipate unexpected opportunities and coincidences, to seize chances that present themselves, and 'to move with the world'. Such skills are not learnt at one's workplace. Nowadays, workers acquire such abilities by living in a big city, gaining aesthetic experiences, having social relationships and networking.[149]

To move with the world (and attain skills, knowledge, aesthetic experience and collaborative networks in the process) stands for specific skills that are, of course, connected to cognitive work. To move with the world can also be understood as a specific exploitation of the human abilities of movement. The relational aspect of movement is at the centre of today's exploitation. The movement of the body is therefore exteriorised; it no longer dwells inside the body as was the case in twentieth century Fordism, where the interiorisation of the movement enabled one to be a part of the larger social machine. Today's subjectivities are flexible because its bodies are organised by means of constant protocols of the acceleration and organisation of everyday and common movement. This kind of distribution enables experimentation with temporality, whereby change is accelerated and spectral. There is no time for hesitation when you move with the world.

The result is a typical form of contemporary subjectivisation or rather desubjectivisation, confronted with the brutal intensification of the processes of individuation, with old forms of life becoming obsolete even before we are able to absorb them. One is therefore compelled to live in a constant state of tension on the verge of despair. Such intensification would not be possible without the exteriorization of movement, in which the interrelation of movement is continuously manipulated and regulated by the protocols of the contemporary society of control. Any potential for change dwindles into ineffective, spectral flexibility. As a result, human subjectivity becomes a source of many possibilities without any influence on reality.

There is something deeply choreographic about today's social machine, which discloses its own compositions through the constant organisation of smoothness, acceleration, non-disturbance and the illusion that movement has nothing to do with disturbance. The material for this kind of social choreography comes from what bodies can do: their everyday mobility and numerous movements through numerous protocols of transgression, which are heavily controlled and regulated. One of the basic illusions of the contemporary subject is that we only move due to an inner feeling of time. This illusion serves as a basis for constantly subduing contemporary subjectivity to numerous apparatuses that promise an ever greater mobility to defeat our ontological slowness. The time of the subject is not a homogeneous time projecting into the future, i.e. a possibility that constantly needs to be realised. Rather, it is about constantly avoiding obstacles, involuntary movement, and slowness that makes time run out.

This makes contemporary dance a political field where proposals within the human ability to move can be explored and connected to the broader social and political reality. In this sense, it needs to bring together the two politics of twentieth century dance: dancing and walking. Subversive pleasure comes from the distance that the dancing body has towards the institutional mechanisms of the exteriorisation of movement, precisely because it can dance. In this sense, the ability to move can resist the economic and social organisation of the relational aspect of movement and open up other embodied ways of moving together that continuously create flows of disturbances and affective persistence.

With its various rhythms, movement can create tensions and put pressure on the seemingly smooth protocols of the contemporary capitalistic world. Today, this need for the moving body is quite apparent in the changed protest strategies such as the 'Occupy' movements, which switched from disembodied networks and global movements to localised but connected forms of temporal persistence and endurance in certain places – to a durational search for new political embodiments. That is why this pleasure can create radical political disruption even if it belongs to the quantitative organisation and distribution of bodies. This pleasure needs to be linked with the ability of everyday movement to induce change, in the ways in which we should think of movement as a qualitative disturbance, a constant changing of the forces of life, a temporal dynamics and materiality of space. This pleasure springs from the fact that movement can induce change, that it can function as an important point of differentiation between spectral change and change that directly affects the body and its relations to the world.

If this is the case, we need to ask the following important question: what exactly do we do when we work – or more precisely, what do we do when we work with dance? The political potentiality of dance is not connected to the space outside work, where the body is free to move and disclose its potentiality of being in time and space; it needs to be placed in dialogue with the modes of flexible production and non-material contemporary work.

It is well-known that the production of contemporary dance is becoming flexible today due to constant movement, in which the exchange of forever young and forever experimental artists (a cheap labour force for the increasingly globalised performance market) goes hand in hand with spectacular shows in order to encourage collaboration for collaboration's sake, and with the continuous movement of the labour force being unavoidable. We tend to forget that there is a materiality to dance and movement, not only that of the body but also that of time and space. It is not abstract and does not rush into the spectral kinetic flow; it is also graspable, located, stuck, partial, rough and ill-timed. This materiality resists the contemporaneity of time and somehow sabotages the spectral appearance of 'the now'; it gives a different rhythm to the flow of time. This materiality can also be connected to the materiality of work in general; dance is very close to work issues in this sense as well.

Dance is not close to work issues because it can function as a representation of work or an image of the working process, but because it *is* work in terms of its material rhythms, efforts and the ways in which it inhabits space and time. It is work in the sense that bodies distribute themselves in space and time, relate to each other and spend or expand their energies. Therefore, the political potentiality of dance should not be searched for in the abstract or democratic idea of freedom and infinite potentiality of movement, but in the ways in which dance is deeply intertwined with the power and exhaustion of work, with its virtuosity and failure, dependence and autonomy. In that sense, dance practice of the last few decades has been stressing its own ontological propositions (e.g. dance equals movement; production and collaboration in dance; the relationship between dance and theory).

All these propositions testify to the fact that dance practice is strongly aware of the relationship between dance and work. If dance is work (and not something opposite to it, in which dance is finally liberated from the materiality of work), then the political potentiality of dance can also be understood as an interesting repetition or replacement of the avant-garde gesture: what would the proposition that dance is work mean for the society that is still to come? Is it possible to find an alternative to the continuous movement and speed, to the flexibility of bodies and spaces, to the dispersion of the energies and power of bodies congregating only due to advertising campaigns and massive spectacles?

One of the possible answers would be the following: dance can reveal that kinetic sensibility not only flows, but opens up caesuras, antagonisms and unbridgeable differences. In this sense, many of the dance performances of the last decade have called for a connection between movement and dance as well as for a broadening of the notion of choreography. Another answer would be that the materiality of dance can resist the abstracted notion of work and reveal the problematic connection between the abstracted new work modes and bodies. New work modes namely have a tremendous power over bodies, especially since they increasingly erase every representable and imaginable generality of bodies. The dancing body no longer resists dull working conditions and does not search for a new society outside work; it can have the power to reveal that the materiality of bodies distributed in time and space can change the ways we live and work together. This politically and aesthetically transgressive line between work and non-work can open up the potential ways of the society of the future.

4.2. Slowing down Movement

In order to understand how movement is connected with change and how this opens numerous ways of contemporary perception, it is necessary to think of movement in its relation to time. On 17th November 2007, in one of their *Ballettikka Internettikka* guerrilla actions, which intervened into various spaces using robots and other miniature mechanical devices for a decade, and broadcast these events online, Igor Štromajer and Brane Zorman illegally brought a robot to the top of the famous Lippo Centre in Hong Kong. On the other side of the world, at an equally eminent avant-garde art venue, the Hellerau Festival House in Dresden (Germany), the audience was waiting for the broadcast of this 'illegal' guerrilla ballet action, which was scheduled for 10

PM CET. The steps of the action and the schedule of the preparations for the ballet were planned up to the minute, in accordance with the illegal nature of the event. Temporality came second to the strategic effect of taking over the space and synchronicity served the realization of the planned event.

Through a series of short electronic messages from the two authors, the audience was notified in advance about all the details of the action and the ascent of the Hong Kong skyscraper, on top of which *Ballettikka Internettikka: Stattikka* – an 'almost static but still transitive net ballet' was supposed to take place. At 10 PM, giant projections began in the Hellerau Hall. On its walls, ceiling and floor, the image of the robot appeared. With two red lights as eyes, the robot was situated on a concrete edge made of white ceramic tiles, as though it were just about to take a new step. Behind it, one could see the glittering and rhythmically pulsating lights of the Hong Kong metropolis, a night without proper darkness. Throughout, there was a sound as though someone were continually changing the (local) radio stations. The length of the transmission was determined in advance: 35 minutes. After the first two minutes, the head technician in charge of the transmission to the hall skyped the two authors atop the Hong Kong skyscraper: "Hey, is everything ok? When will things start? There's nothing happening here yet."[150] The authors replied that everything was fine. After 35 minutes of transmission, a meticulously scheduled and synchronised descent took place, followed by securing the equipment. The level of risk involved in the action was assessed as the maximum by the two authors.

Indeed, when are things going to start? The question of the technician in charge of the connection between Dresden and Hong Kong was not that of a person technically skilled but 'uninformed' in the field of contemporary art. Rather, it mirrored the increasingly uncomfortable atmosphere in the hall; after a few minutes, people began to fidget, walk around and many actually left the hall. The artistic director of the festival, Johannes Birringer, later described the various reactions of the audience in his blog. While some people were enthusiastically following the authors' project, others almost meditatively yielded themselves to the transmission on the screens, and still others felt a deep frustration, perhaps even anger, and left the hall in protest. After the performance, Birringer's blog also featured a discussion between the authors of the transmission and some members of the audience. The general findings could be summed up in two points: a) that not much happened; and b) that if the audience had been more informed about the context of the performance, they might have been more accepting of the 'considerable or complete lack of goings-on'. The reaction of the audience testifies to the fact that duration can be problematic, especially in a technological context: if duration becomes independent, it needs a context. It needs to be filled with something before its slowness begins to get to us – we simply need to know *why* things have stopped.

Ballettikka Internettikka: Stattikka could be classified as a networked performance, i.e., a performance that broadcasts a real time and space event over the Internet, which, in *Ballettikka*'s case, featured a mechanical robot/toy as the main dancer. For these reasons, the performance raises quite a few issues related to the relationship between duration and barely perceptible movement. *Ballettikka* was part of Tele-Plateaus, a festival programme that, by means of broadcasts from various parts of the world, attempted to open up a platform for experimentation with synchronous temporalities and reflect on new event concepts established by the relations between technology and performance.[151] One might expect that duration, the expansion of the event, cannot intrigue an audience that is used to performances where the time dimension is heavily experimented with (the perception of time by the audience, etc.). In *Ballettikka Internettikka: Stattikka* something paradoxical takes place. The connection works and the broadcast is successful, but it seems as though something went wrong; there is duration, but it comes across like a failure; there is slowness, but it seems as though it resulted from some sort of technical malfunction.

Placed on the white-tiled edge with the city view behind it, the robot/toy is not moving, but it is being transmitted. In this way, it embodies the very title of the performance – static ballet. Although the event is broadcast successfully, it seems as though the connection was not working, and we could quickly begin to feel that this unique 'non-event' is wasting our time.

When something does not function (the body, a machine, a car, a computer, a vending machine), the duration literally intervenes into the subject that witnesses this halt. It seems as though our inner sense of time was appropriated by the non-functioning machine; the subject suddenly feels that he/she has been dispossessed – and needs to slow down and wait. This slowing down and waiting is frequently felt in contemporary culture when the dispositives that regulate and organize our flexible subjectivities no longer work: for example, the protocols of moving through the city, social networks, airports, motorways, mobile phones. These kinds of halts in motion or slow-downs have a direct influence on the body as they appropriate the temporality of the subject, organized as endless flexibility, simultaneity and adaptability in today's times. In moments like this, we say that we are stuck, with little else to do but hang in there and become powerless observers of our own chronological time. According to Agamben, time flies by for observers of their own chronological time; they are never left with any of it and always miss their own selves.[152] All the dispositives we use to establish ourselves as subjects today promise speed and effectiveness, not only in our actions but also in our subjectivisation processes. The greater the speed promised by the dispositives, the less tolerant and the more affective our responses become when something remains stationary instead of working. Most of us feel agitated within several seconds when a desired computer programme does not open; we feel like giving the computer a smack, just like we used to do with the old televisions when the image was flickering and unstable. When something is stopped, it seems as though our subjectivity of the one stopped will be disabled, as though it will be dispossessed. Perhaps the affective response is a consequence of the fact that it is duration that shows that we ourselves are actually not moving, but are being moved, that our inner perception of time (the time of someone who freely and flexibly projects their own subjectivity) is in fact heavily socially and economically conditioned.

In many of their projects, Igor Štromajer and Brane Zorman purposefully contrast mutually exclusive temporalities. On the one hand, the almost 'theatrical' preparation for the event (which cannot be seen during the transmission) gains a classic dramaturgical structure through the constant acceleration and division of the time of the action. On the other hand, the live broadcast of the event is a long way from the accumulated and anticipated effect. The artists contrast two exclusive temporalities that can also be understood as the two basic inner temporal qualities of the contemporary flexible subject. On the one hand, the subject today is fully subjugated to the concept of accelerated time and organized through precise time management of its actions and movement; everything (including human potentiality) is organized in time sequences that are supposed to lead to a certain effect. On the other hand, the inner time of the subject can also be described as an escalation of redundant time (time in which we are stuck), slowness, motionlessness, stasis and non-functioning. In this way, *Ballettikka Internettikka: Stattikka* mirrors an interesting dynamic in the contemporary experience of temporality, where the activity of the subject constantly intertwines with fatigue. At the very moment when the clock begins to tick and the hall is illuminated on the other side of the planet, the investment of the two authors in the event (on both the concrete and phantasmagorical levels, which makes the audience eager in its expectations) is flattened into the static but transitive image of movement that has stopped, a still image. The investment, the entire preparation for the event, becomes consumption without an effect, a waste of energy and actions to produce an effect that is too slow, a 'lesser effect', so to speak. There is a specific incapability at work in relation to the expectation of what could happen in *Ballettikka*, a specific exhaustion of the event itself.

This dynamic of action and fatigue could also be compared to the economic relationship between the time of the investment and the time of the consumption. The time of the investment, although flexible and multi-layered, is also homogenous. Today, time is structured in a projective manner: one needs to achieve an effect and realize future goals. This directly contributes to the (subjective) feeling of time acceleration. At the same time, the consumption of investments has become too plentiful and is downright redundant. Not only does it have harmful effects on our habitat (natural or social), but also underlies the experience of subjectivity as redundancy, dissatisfaction, insufficient gains, a phantasmagorical waste of energy and resources that brings exhaustion instead of an affirmation of subjectivity.[153] The subject's crisis therefore springs from this excessive dynamic of investment and consumption, where the body of the subject is frequently taken over by fatigue, a form of stillness that comes directly from excessive speed: in our culture, speed and slowness seem to be in direct and traumatic opposition. In all its formations, especially those playing with the contexts of break-in and illegality, *Ballettikka* plays with these feelings of time organization through expectation and the consumption of time – with the expectation of the event and its actual realisation.

Similar feelings are triggered by *NVSBL* (2007), a dance performance by Eszter Salamon. This is just one of a number of dance performances where movement has been reduced to a minimum; it has analogous qualities to the unsuccessful movement of the robot in the video projected in the Hellerau Hall. It is true that this performance features the barely perceptible movement of live bodies; however, there is something comparable in the way in which the bodies are slowed down inside a decelerated image, as they would be if recorded in slow motion. The title of the performance is deliberately without consonants; the word itself resembles the movement in an image broadcast with a delay effect. Very slowly, four dancers appear from the background, motionless and yet moving. Their bodies seem to slide from one flickering image to another, but cannot actually be retained in the memory. A comparison could easily be made with a broadcast where the image is unstable, delayed and the transmission is not functioning properly.

The performance, which is difficult to describe without reducing it to the logic of the events, has been captured by the philosopher Cristina Demaria in the following way: "On stage we watch the imperceptible and therefore invisible movements of four dancers who emerge very slowly from a dark background: with their bodies, and with a miraculous play of lights, they are not so much composing figures as being figures, apparently motionless but actually changing. Figures that become channels of a 'logic of sensation' (Deleuze), at times also laboriously alienating for a public accustomed to seeing and therefore judging what it manages to interpret ('But nothing's happening here,' said a woman in front of me, fidgeting nervously in her seat). It is a logic capable of restoring our thought of the body as a force at once precise and devastating and also, quite simply, beautiful, like the beauty associated with certain paintings that continually come to mind as we try to watch NVSBL. The power of this thought is demonstrated by such a reduction of movement in space as to render the very reality of the bodies inaccessible, because it deprives us of control over our own perception and consequently of presumed control over bodies which our vision believed it could frame and interpret with its own memory models."[154] This description is close to what I would define as the potentiality of duration: the reduction and absence of movement are so radical that they shatter the reality of the bodies and, at the same time, dispossess our perception.

Time becomes independent when it does not allow us to fill emptiness with meaning. In this performance, the images are structured in such a way that they do not allow us to focus on anything and retain things in our memory; time is so redundant that it takes control over our perception. The consequence of this temporal redundancy is the dispossession of our inner sense of time, whereby our attention no longer empowers our subjective experience. Quite the opposite: we are stuck, duration disables us, it takes over. When we are overwhelmed with a redundancy of time, duration does not stimulate our attention and does not enable a more intense awareness of the subject. Attention becomes rather impersonal, as described by Blanchot: "It is not the self that is attentive in attention; rather, with an extreme delicacy and through insensible, constant contacts, attention has always already detached me from myself, freeing me for the attention that I for an instant become."[155] This is why duration does not stimulate our attention, activate us and make us more sensitive and open – more self-aware. Duration has nothing to do with tension. Quite the opposite is the case: during redundant time that is running out, we are stuck, with our attention waiting.

It is only when we approach duration as something that is related to the dispossession of subjectivity that it can be discussed as a potentially critical concept in contemporary culture. The two aforementioned works help us gain an insight into the current cultural and political dimensions of duration, which have different critical properties than the experiments with duration and temporality in the second half of the twentieth century.

In contemporary theatre, the stretching of time has long been at the forefront. For example, Lehmann writes that, in contemporary theatre, we often no longer speak of the representation of the timeline, but about the presentation in its own temporality. Duration in theatre does not portray duration; in other words; when the performance slows down, the slowness on stage does not refer to the slowness of the fictitious universe, which is supposed to fuse with our own experiential world. Temporality becomes an immanent 'conscious' element of the performance, by means of which theatre refers to its own process. This means that the experience of time expansion and, consequently, the various strategies for organizing the spectator's diffused perception are at the forefront. Theatre takes place and is organised in the gap between its fictitious time and the time of the audience.[156] Instead of representing homogenous time (dramatic time, the time of the subject, the time of the event, etc.), contemporary theatre takes place as a heterogeneity of temporalities, where a coherent temporality no longer exists. The performances experiment with time and the attention of the spectator; they break up the sequence and coherence of the events, experiment with memories and things that are yet to come, with repetition, with phenomenological experience, etc.

In this way, theatre has frequently been understood as the artistic field that defies the strict rationalization and effectiveness of homogenous time in contemporary capitalist society, enabling the parallel and heterogeneous experience of attention, and revealing the incoherence of the subject (e.g. Lehmann). When the temporal experience of the subject cannot be embraced as a coherent unit, but as a flexible, heterogeneous and contradictory one, the subject cannot be subjugated by the social organizational structures and the subject's experience of time is not subdued into effectiveness. In this way, contemporary performance seems to offer resistance to the social division of time and the understanding of time as a means of economic effectiveness (where time is considered as economic value). As Adrian Heathfield writes, the theatre experiments of the early 1970s that introduce duration by means of various procedures (repetition, the expansion of the performance beyond the cultural convention, improvisation, coincidence and the non-materiality of the event) establish a critical understanding of time as a commodity and create unassailable values that cannot be subjugated by the existing social and cultural constructions of time, where time is closely connected to the effectiveness and rationalization of the social systems.[157]

In the early 1970s, when theatre experiments brought duration into performance by means of various procedures, changes began to take place in the manner of subjectivisation in the wider social and cultural spheres that could be linked with emerging post-industrial society. The changes were connected with what was discussed by the Italian philosophers who detected deep changes in social organization. The difference between work and free time is disappearing; the communicative and linguistic dimension is at the forefront; human potentiality is at the core of production. The power of production becomes the thing that establishes us as human beings, as potent beings. This shift causes important changes in social organization and the cultural concepts of time.

Experimenting with time (simultaneousness, heterogeneity, synchronicity) is at the forefront, accompanied by play with time compression, crisis and release (both on the personal and social levels). Experimenting with time serves to enhance the effectiveness and production value of the subject, as well as the value of virtual predictions and projections (not only in the financial market, but also in social structures). As contradictory as it may sound, experimenting with time is what contributes to the subduing of the contemporary flexible subject. Time experimentation is an essential condition for the value of work itself.

Let's try to find evidence for this argument in contemporary artistic and cultural production. Most of those active in this field are involved with projecting projects and realizing those projected projects. The time dimension is already contained in the term 'project': actions in the future, the actualisation of possibilities, etc. Despite the fact that experimenting and constant movement is at their core, projects are simultaneously part of a homogenous temporality that we feel as an intense acceleration at both the intimate and social levels. The heterogeneous character of projects, which involve exceptional human abilities, belong to an all-embracing homogenous temporality that does not enable a different social model of organization even though, paradoxically, it needs to constantly invent them in order for the project to succeed.[158]

My question would therefore be as follows: what is the critical value of duration in the post-industrial situation, where the inner feeling of the subject increasingly fuses with the value of his/her productivity and where the heterogeneity of temporality is at the core of shaping contemporary subjectivity? What is the critical value of duration if the heterogeneity of time is part of the subduing of the subject, the appropriation of the subject's worth by the economy?

I see an essential difference in the following fact. A few decades ago, duration could be understood as a sort of visibility of activity (process, structure, immediacy, failure, coincidence, redundancy), and a way to manage the attention of the spectator and her/his sensibility. In the second half of the twentieth century, duration is therefore closely connected to the entry of work into the performance itself (e.g. improvisation in dance, where decisions are made in the present and the work is not hidden behind the dancing body) and to the emancipation of the performance process. Interestingly, this entry and visibility of work processes in the performance runs parallel to the new methods of post-industrial production, where work is no longer Fordist as a rule, but increasingly virtuosic. It takes place before others, i.e. the audience, and acquires increasingly communicative features.

Today, due to changes in the inner perception of time, which is so closely connected with the contemporary dispositives of multi-temporality, heterogeneity and flexibility, I feel that we need to think in the direction of duration as a dispossession that overwhelms us with non-functioning and non-operativity. In order for the subjects to last, they need to be literally dispossessed, forget themselves as a subject.[159] This is why even short time units can have a very long duration today. Due to the accelerated and projective character of our inner time, subjects find themselves in a no man's land if something does not function or if nothing is going on; they feel as though the duration intrudes upon them and, paradoxically, steals the most intimate time.

Duration, gives nothing in return; it does not sharpen our senses and nor do we acquire a different sensibility or intensiveness by yielding to it. Duration does not activate us; it only dispossesses us and fails to catch our attention. In the two aforementioned performances, duration does not cause sublime effects; if the performances do not irritate us so much that we leave immediately, we are suddenly stuck. We sit there in the midst of the performance and do not surrender to its flow, only try and get through it as though it were an obstacle, actually having to move through it step by step. Our attention waits "without precipitation, leaving empty what is empty and keeping our haste, our impatient desire, and, even more, our horror of emptiness from prematurely filling it up."[160]

Culturally, duration can be deeply subversive, but not because it contrasts the experience of slowness with the experience of speed (after all, slow movement is a privilege of the rich and an inevitable for the poor). Duration irritates us because it can reveal how deeply our most intimate perception of time (i.e. the feeling that we are active beings and constantly on the move) is socially constructed and economically conditioned. For this reason, duration demolishes social and organisation protocols; the time we have needs to dispossess us in order for us to be able to last. Since our daily life calls for ubiquitous and constant actualisation, duration does not enable actualisation, but quite the opposite. It places us into a state of pure potentiality, into what is still supposed to come. While lasting, we wait for time to run out. This dispossession through duration is not only characteristic of contemporary art; we can trace it in the arts to the 1960s onwards, where duration is at the forefront of numerous artistic experiments of live art, performance and film.[161]

By experimenting with duration and movement, the two performances I have described open up the problematics of dispossession, not because nothing is happening, but because the redundant time generated interferes heavily with the inner processes of subjectivisation: we are suddenly left with time, which means that being is potentially possible without self-actualization. This description also has concrete political and cultural implications. Slow observation that does not concentrate upon the actual effect, the dispossession in which we create something before it actually happens, characterises the manner of working in contemporary theatre and dance. This is especially true if performance is understood as the field of experimenting with and critically addressing the social and economic contexts in which we live and work. Duration also directly sabotages the organization of the social protocols of flexibility and mobility, especially when we are speaking of duration as a specific relationship with movement. Contrastingly, continuous and accelerated movement (described by Sloterdijk as kinetic modernity)[162], expels any kind of potency from the actualisation of the subject: professions need to be changed quickly, everything needs to be made usable, the future needs to be organized into a projection. Duration reveals that movement does not only belong to the activity of the subject; we only begin to last when moved by others – when we have been placed into the world.

Finally, let me illustrate the concept of duration with one

more image, a personal one from my former home city. It is an image of the view from the window of one of my previous homes. I lived near an old people's home, whose residents took walks in a small circular park, where one could do little but repeat the path over and over. Whenever I looked at the park through my window, I felt that something had changed in my perception of time. In the clamour of the city, a movement was revealed that could be looked at without a kinaesthetic feeling being triggered in my body. The duration of the people's walks shows itself as the slowness of the body no longer capable of the continuous and invisible transition of the city inhabitant. However, the walks the old people take always confirm to me that movement is not only about crossing a space, getting from point A to point B. This is also discussed by Deleuze: "Movement is not a unity of quantitative differences that can be endlessly multiplied."[163]

Such is our global movement of today. Our subjectivity is organised as a unity of quantitative differences marked by an endless acceleration of the numeric differences between the places we have visited, the residences we have inhabited and the people we are connected with. Movement is not only a transient movement in space, but should also be understood as change, as quantitative differentiation. For example, Deleuze refers to the eminent philosophical parable of the fearless runner Achilles; despite his youth and strength, his movement resembles that of the old people in the park, who would represent the turtle in this parable. It is not about equal speed, but about an equal mode of duration. Achilles's movement can be quantitatively divided into steps; with every step, the movement changes in a qualitative way. Deleuze says: "What seems from the outside to be a numerical part, a component of the run, turns out to be, experienced from the inside, an obstacle avoided."[164] The inner perception of movement is therefore quantitative and enables change, precisely because movement concerns us from the outside.

The interesting thing about those no longer young bodies taking their walks might be precisely that the experience of movement as qualitative change shows on the surface of the body. Movement is a relationship. It constantly dispossesses us by means of obstacles that we cannot react to if we wish to move. One of the basic illusions of the contemporary subject is that we only move because of our inner feeling of time. This illusion also serves as a basis for constantly subduing contemporary subjectivity to an increasing number of dispositives that promise even greater mobility to defeat our ontological slowness.

The time of the subject is therefore not a homogenous projecting time, a possibility that constantly needs to be realised. Rather, it is constantly avoiding obstacles, involuntary movement, a slowness in which time itself is running out. The German anthropologist and philosopher Odo Marquard writes that the obsession with speed in contemporary culture can also be understood as an incessant acceleration of the speed of life, a response to the ontological fact of the shortness of human life. Marquard claims that, in comparison to death, all human life is fundamentally slow. Only in this way can we bear the shortness of human life in comparison to the world around it, the fact that we are but a "niche in time".[165] Human beings need to have a sense of slowness because this is the only way to differentiate those changes that are desired and possible. Maybe that's why the relation between duration and movement is so important: it enables a waiting in which we look at something that is not yet there.

Chapter 5

The Visibility of Work

5.1. The Artist as a Virtuoso

A few years ago, the Belgian philosopher Dieter Lesage was invited to collaborate with the artist Ina Wudtke on writing an introductory text for her catalogue. Lesage took the invitation seriously; rather than describing her artistic "products", his *"Portrait of the Artist as a Worker"* meticulously describes what Wudtke actually does when she works as an artist. "You are an artist and that means: you don't do it for the money. That is what some people think. It is a great excuse not to pay you for all the things you do. So what happens is that you, as an artist, put money into projects that others will show in their museum, in their Kunsthalle, in their exhibition space, in their gallery. So you are an investor. You give loans nobody will repay you. You take financial risks. You speculate on yourself as an artistic asset. You are a trader. You cannot put all your money into one kind of artistic stock. So you diversify your activities. You manage the risks you take. You would say it differently. I know. You say you suffer from a gentle schizophrenia. You have multiple personalities. You are a photographer, but also a DJ. You have a magazine, you are a publisher, but you also organize parties. You take photos of party people. You throw a party when you present a magazine, you make magazines with photographs of party people, you throw a party and you are the DJ. You do interviews with people you meet, you do interviews with people you would like to meet, you tell the people you meet about your magazine. You buy records on flea markets, you distribute flyers announcing parties in the bar where you have a coffee after visiting the flea market, you make videos recording how you destroy the records you bought on the flea market, you liberate your country from its bad music, you show the video in a gallery and you are a DJ at the vernissage."[166]

By meticulously enumerating her multiple activities, which move between organization, production, dissemination, networking, the presentation of the artwork and the artist herself, in a fast repetitive rhythm, Lesage directly indicates the profound changes in the work of the contemporary artist that have been taking place over the last few decades. By shifting the focus from *artistic work* to *the artist's work*, i.e. from aesthetic or philosophical reflection on the work to its actual production, Lesage not only attempts to draw attention to what the artist has to do as an artist, but also to show that the manner in which artists work is strongly intertwined with the way artistic work is valued and recognized today. He shows that the open, interdisciplinary, unstable and flexible character of contemporary artistic work is not only an aesthetic quality but one deeply connected to the ways how the works are produced.

Ina Wudtke moves between various production activities, changes the methods of creating, makes recordings, holds meetings, writes presentation materials, edits applications, re-records things, takes presentation photos, holds some more meetings, organizes parties, transgresses between numerous project preparations and realizations. Her work is highly flexible and mobile, taking place simultaneously at different levels. It is impossible to differentiate between her artistic work and its presentation, between the making of the work and its public dissemination, or between the materiality and non-materiality of the artistic work. It is also impossible to draw a line between her numerous activities, her professional and private lives, the creation and organization of her work, the creativity and advertising of her work, or her work and her pleasure. All her activities are united into a single all-encompassing current flowing cyclically through Lesage's meticulous description of every single 'banal detail' of her work.

Ina Wudtke's portrait is that of a top-notch virtuoso. Not only does she create virtuosic work, her performance of the work surrounding the artistic work is virtuosic as well. She is a virtuoso in *the way* she works. Her portrait reveals a top-notch virtuosity in all the aspects and nuances of her work as a contemporary artist. Lesage compares her virtuosity to that of a DJ, and this comparison is not coincidental. Ina Wudtke actually works as a DJ and a visual artist; this makes her work comparable to that of other performing artists, e.g. musicians, actors and speakers, whose work is virtuosic due to the absence of a final product. The aim of their activities is not the creation of a product, but the performance itself. Furthermore, Wudtke's work always takes place before the eyes of other people, in the presence of an audience. Her virtuosity is about performing a specific 'score', which not only includes her 'musical work' but her activities in their entirety. In this sense, her activities can be viewed as a corroboration of Paolo Virno's thesis that, in a post-Fordist society, activity without an end product becomes the prototype of any kind of wage work. Contemporary post-Fordist work is predominantly of a communication and linguistic type, taking place continuously before the eyes of others, which adds a basic political trait to its character.[167]

A number of Wudtke's activities are connected to this visibility of work and to the work taking place before the eyes of the audience; this goes for both her non-artistic and her artistic work, which cannot be clearly differentiated. The virtuosity does not only apply to creating music or visual installations; highlighted in Lesage's description is another activity, that of rendering DJ procedures (sampling, recombination, remixing and other music creation processes) into transgression between various qualities and forms of immaterial work: creation by means of materials, communication, presentation materials, meetings, exchange, collaboration, reflection, travelling, recording, re-recording, selling, advertising, project planning etc.

In this way, Lesage also differs from Bourriaud's claim about the artist as a contemporary DJ who rhetorically translates these procedures into the reuse of forms and a reprogramming of the procedures through which today's artistic works supposedly intermediate between forms, signs and images.[168] Ina Wudtke's portrait shows that the artist is actually an ideal virtuoso of contemporary post-Fordist work; indeed, she demonstrates top-notch skills in its various aspects (flexibility, mobility, performativity, simultaneity, impermanence). Despite the fact that her work belongs to the post-Fordist way of working, her work is highly repetitive and ceaseless, i.e. similar to the Fordist assembly line in terms of rhythm. Lesage indicates the complex status of contemporary virtuosity which, also according to Virno, characterizes the entire social production of today; the most important aspect of social production are the linguistic and communicative performances, in which the aforementioned score is just that of general intellect (in terms of the general human faculty of communication and community building). "Nobody is as poor as those who see their own relation to the presence of others, that is to say, their own communicative faculty, their own possession of a language, reduced to wage labor."[169]

If we wish to delve deeper into the topical closeness of art and capitalism, we therefore need to focus on *visibility*, an important characteristic of today's artistic work. The vanishing dividing line between artistic work and work itself needs to be rethought; in many artistic practices, this phenomenon is connected to the disappearing dividing line between life and art. In the continuation, I will show that the artist in contemporary society has become a prototype of the contemporary flexible and precarious worker because the artist's work is connected to the production of life itself – in other words, with the production of subjectivity and the excess of sociality as discussed in previous chapters.

Today, the vanishing dividing line between life and work,

placed by many twentieth-century artists at the core of their emancipation tendencies is also at the centre of the capitalist processes of life exploitation. It often seems that the artist is the ideal worker in contemporary capitalism; it is also no coincidence that the artistic lifestyle and the exploitation of life as an endless creative process underlie the speculation on the future value of art. Contemporary artistic subjectivity enters the critical analyses of post-Fordist capitalist culture due to the disappearance of the borders between the 'artistic work' and the way the work is made: placed at the forefront is the immateriality of artistic work, its event-related and relational component, where the borders between the process and the product become blurred. Notably, there is a contradiction in all this: the procedures of bringing art and life closer together (in the twentieth century, their main aim was to open the emancipation potential of art and to shift the focus to the process of creation by detaching from the materiality of the artistic object) are now at the core of the capitalist creation of value.

Interestingly, numerous theatrical and dance performances of the last few decades have thematised their own work procedures, which have often been viewed as an expansion of the artistic field itself (choreography, dance, performance art) moving the traditional borders of art. This has been especially true of European contemporary dance since the 1990s; the field has been strongly marked by the introduction of the visibility of the labour itself, especially aspects not necessarily connected to physical endeavours but with the new affective atmospheres and energetic tensions of work. These new work procedures have indeed been able to bridge the traditional role hierarchies (e.g. the relationship between the choreographer and the dancer, between the artist and the institution, etc.) and contribute to broadening the perspective in terms of what specifically artistic practices can still become (what dance can be, what the body can do); they have also contributed to changing the artistic institutions into more community- and experiment-oriented spaces. Nevertheless, these new work procedures have also been closely connected with new post-Fordist ways of production. This is why it is necessary to rethink the 'political traits' of the new ways of working and point out the contradictions of the flexible, non-material processes in art – especially the ways in which the visibility of work is part of contemporary processes of work exploitation.

Discussions on the closeness of artistic and capitalist work already began at the end of the 1990s, especially under the influence of Luc Boltanski and Eve Chiapello, whose book *The New Spirit of Capitalism* highlights the similarities between artistic subjectivity and the subjectivity of contemporary capitalism.[170] Frequently understood as the ideal subjectivity of contemporary capitalism, especially in connection with the rise of the creative class, artistic subjectivity is by no means lazy and inactive; quite the opposite, it is incessantly active in all its possible forms and in the realization of its potentiality. According to Boltanski and Chiapello, autonomy, self-realization, creativity and the disappearance of the difference between work time and private time are characteristics of contemporary creative work at the core of the new spirit of capitalism.

The authors analyse the powerlessness and collapse of institutional art criticism, which arose from the emancipation tendencies in the 1960s and the affirmation of the shift after 1968. In their opinion, one of the reasons for the powerlessness of art criticism after the 1960s was the consent to and contentment with the changes that introduced the management concepts of flexibility, mobile creativity, the open process and creative participation into the ways of working, and which placed an emphasis on the linguistic and performative dimensions of the working process. We could therefore conclude that many contemporary characteristics of the creative artistic processes (openness, exploration, the increasing closeness of art and life) can also be found in the new work processes that appeared along with post-Fordism. The exploitation of potentiality, communication abilities and flexibility (constant availability) of the working subject, the entry of virtuosity into the workplace, the vanishing difference between work and free time, the increase in the performative ability of the contemporary worker – all this intertwines with the projective creation of new forms and contexts, as well as with the performative orientation of every segment of work.[171]

Located at the core of contemporary work is visible work (labour), performed before the eyes of other people. Consequently, every evaluation and judgment of work is connected to this visible core, to experimentation and the development of the subject's linguistic, affective and imaginative abilities. The visibility of work is closely connected to what Virno describes as the increasing closeness of work and political activity. This visibility of work is also at the heart of the managerial, unfinished (projective) nature and openness of work; here aesthetic characteristics of work and their appropriation by contemporary production processes are closely intertwined.

Let's return to Ina Wudtke's portrait. Her work is open, processual, precarious and continually moving between different activities; this is not only true of her 'bureaucratic and managerial work', but also of her artistic work, which is closely connected to its production apparatus. This apparatus is abstract in the sense that immateriality is a trait of both the artistic work and the work process. The process is primarily geared towards what the work could be, aiming for the exchange of the potentiality of work (the production of contexts, meanings, transfers etc.); the work takes place in the form of speculation on the work itself.[172] As an artist, Ina Wudtke must be constantly networking, she has to be communicative and virtuosic; she must be skilled at numerous creative ways of making her work visible. It is through this process that her artistic work is created in the first place.

Lesage therefore points out that there is an interesting economic connection between her labour and artistic work, one calling for artistic work to be analysed together with its production: in fact, this is the only way in which an aesthetic analysis of artistic work can actually be made. The production of artistic work concerns the open and creative processes that can take place parallel to the radical exploitation of the work in general. It is not so much about the analysis of the institutional working conditions, but about the ways in how the art work is actually produced.

Contemporary artistic institutions are also part of this flexibility and speculation with work, with even the most progressive ones collaborating in the exploitation of a poorly paid and flexible work force; even the most self-critical artistic institutions actually generate the same economic and social models that they criticize in their works. The artistic decisions, methods and aesthetic traits of the artistic work are closely connected to its production conditions; the way we work is deeply ingrained in the form of our artistic work. Artistic institutions like to consider themselves progressive, but many of them are only able to survive due to the exploitation of flexible and non-payed work; the organization apparatus/bureaucratic management is actually organized as a series of internships, residences and extensions of endless education. Frequently, this free, precarious, barely paid and flexible work sees no difference between free time and working time. This work is surrounded by a certain social aura in terms of the symbolic value of the artistic institution as a parallel social space, the friendship between its actors and the value of this 'artistic' life in general. This does not mean that institutions need to be moralistically condemned as bad. Their framing within contemporary economic methods of production does need to be noted: they do exist as an important and active part of the shift into precarious and flexible work, in which they also support the affective construction of the precarious understanding of subjectivity.

The functioning of artistic institutions is thus closely connected to the omnipresent feeling of precariousness. Lauren Berlant characterizes this precariousness not only as economic but as structural and thus typical of the contemporary affective environment we live in.[173] In her opinion, this kind of structural precariousness marks the experience of the present moment as well as the atmospheres and rhythms of contemporary life.

The functioning of many contemporary artistic institutions should be read in the light of this affective shift, which hails creativity and temporary freedom as essential but also gives rise to an increasing feeling of powerlessness and instability. According to Berlant, this affective feeling consists of the simultaneous frustration and free delight felt by the educated but rather rarely employed intellectual classes. These classes are characterized by constant mobility, network building and insistence that they are at the centre rather than on the margin of the social. They are characterized by a rhetoric of care for others and the new social ecology, demanding that the state guarantee the basic conditions for the flourishing of their work and mobility (food, clothing, shelter, employment), without any of them having to renounce the flexible, migratory and unstable way of life they have fought out for themselves.[174] This description reminds me of the feeling frequently present at the core of contemporary artistic subjectivity, which also develops a new social ecology of giving and friendship in order to be able to persist in the precarious and unbearable instability of such life in which it closely participates: in the omnipresent affective shift and the exploitation of subjectivity. The progressiveness of the institutions should therefore be connected to these deeply affective and intimate working conditions; this would directly influence the structure and functioning of the institutions and transform the value of our investment into them. Instead of an abstract aura of friendship, the institutions should develop forms of solidarity and permanence of work; they should not allow the same work conditions as elsewhere and worsen the contemporary affective climate.

We are dealing with the ambivalent status of the contemporary artist and their work, a status closely connected to the post-Fordist ways of working and cultural production. In the opinion of some authors, the artist becomes the ideal worker for contemporary capitalism; the artist is actually supposed to serve as the basis on which the contemporary fetishisation of creativity and creative neoliberal flexible subjectivity should be modelled. Indeed, the great majority of contemporary artistic practices adopt an extremely critical stance towards creativity; instead, they establish various processes of collaboration that move away from modernist artistic subjectivity. Despite the resistance, these processes also exist as part of post-Fordist work condition, especially due to their inherent communicativeness: contemporary works are primarily established as discursive, performative and intercommunication fields.

It is not only about work becoming a theme; the visibility of work changes the relationship with the audience, which cooperates in its open procedures. Today, many artistic works exist as communication fields enabling the exchange of knowledge and feelings, where it is possible to enter things (work in progress) that are yet unfinished (and thus shoulder one's part/responsibility), and test the closeness and value of what gets produced. This is why a lot of artistic works include the spectator, who collaborates in the production of a work by working with his/her own communicative, social and production abilities.[175] At the same time, the omnipresent feeling of the precarity and prevalence of non-material work establishes a series of symptoms within the contemporary way of working, which also affects the understanding of artistic subjectivity.

For example, Vassilis Tsianos and Dimitris Papadopoulos state a number of neurotic symptoms that fit in well with the ways artistic subjectivity is understood and felt today: vulnerability (the feeling of flexibility without any kind of form of security), hyperactivity (the imperative to keep up with constant accessibility), simultaneity (the ability to keep up the various rhythms and speeds of various simultaneous activities), recombination (transgressing between different networks/social spaces), post-sexuality and fluent intimacy (the bodily production of indeterminate sexual relations), anxiousness (connected to communication and interaction overload), cunningness (the ability to employ opportunism and tricks) and affective exhaustion (emotional exploitation).[176]

In artistic work, the visibility of work is also connected to the ways in which the production of communication, relationships, relations, affects and non-material goods drives out post-Fordist production (or places it into the hidden and closed zones of the 'invisible' world).[177] Today, many artistic practices face the old but extremely important dilemma indicated by Walter Benjamin in his 1934 lecture *The Author as Producer*. In this essay, Benjamin deals with the issues surrounding the relationship between artistic work and social situation – in other words, how and whether artistic work should respond to the specific social situation in which it is generated: what the relationship should be between its tendency and quality. The eminent answer to this question is given at the very beginning of the text; Benjamin writes that "the correct political tendency includes a literary tendency."[178]

The political is therefore also the aesthetic, where the aesthetic in the political should not be understood as a consequence of the 'right' relationship of art to the production relations of its time (this is not about whether artistic work is reactionary or progressive), but especially as the question of how artistic work is placed within the production relations of its time: "Before I ask: how does a literary work stand in relation to the production of a period, I would like to ask: how does it stand in them? This question aims directly at the function that the work has within the literary relationship of production of a period. In other words, it aims directly at a work's technique (Technik)."[179]

Benjamin's notion of technique refers primarily to the aesthetic quality of work, which is also closely connected to the production process and thus comes close to the notion of technology – i.e. the manner in which the work is produced, its method of production. Benjamin's notion of technique opens the door to direct social analysis and enables materialist analysis of artistic works; at the same time, it dialectically cuts in the sterile opposition between tendency and quality (form and content).

Extremely important for our analysis is the fact that the artistic work must explore the ways in which it is produced – in the case of contemporary art, that would be the post-Fordist (open, flexible, communicative, affective) methods that separate the work from the materiality of the working process. Due to the 'seeming' immateriality of contemporary artistic work, there are numerous artistic works with a revolutionary attitude today that have not really thought through their work or its technique in a truly revolutionary manner.[180] Today, when the methods of production are literally fused with the work itself, when the flexibility and communicativeness of the work processes transgress into the openness of work, and when the exploitation of creativity overlaps with experimentation and research, the artist has actually been called upon to constantly revolutionise the methods of his/her own production.

As a producer, the artist is namely skilled at numerous creative and production techniques that go hand in hand with the development of contemporary capitalism. The revolutionizing and changing of these methods is also connected to the immateriality, abstraction and ephemerality of his work – the traits that actually separate work from materiality and the visible processes of practice that are essential in the production of artistic work. The visibility of artistic work becomes the principal technology of its production, and should be connected to the material and embodied processes that actually enable this visibility. Frequently, the visibility is possible due to the precariousness, flexibility and inconstancy of work in general, due to the fetishisation of non-material and speculative experience as the basic social and communicative experience that can be enabled by artistic work. Therefore it is important for artistic practice to return back to the material aspect of work, to the sensuous and material base of any activity.

5.2. The Female Artist between Work and Life

The artistic work reveals that its politicisation – on the border between life and work, non-work and work, and production and reproduction – has been made very difficult today because the basic contemporary hegemonic representation of work is that of the disappearance of this difference, with artistic subjectivity becoming the central image of this fusion. Artistic subjectivity is actually the most efficient representation of the disappearance of this difference.[181] This does not mean that this difference does not exist and still determines contemporary subjectivity.

"Although the economic field, in a double sense, mobilizes and controls the social realm, the paradigms of capitalist production remain the same. They do not inform the resources of our social lives themselves, even (and especially) if cognitive capitalism has parasitically positioned itself at the side of reproduction. Acceleration and maximizing profit continue to be advanced as the necessary logic of the market. Life itself is subsumed under the rules of efficiency and optimization that were first encountered under the regime of automated industrial work in order to synchronize the body with machines. Today, it is our cognitive capabilities that we are expected to optimize and our self-relation (to our work) that we are expected to correct in the interest of lifelong learning"[182]

According to Marion Von Osten, the politicisation of this

difference between life and work has frequently interested feminist artists, who have paid special attention to this difference due to the nature of their work (e.g. the difference between professional, care and motherhood-related work, or public social work and private household work). As an early example of radical critique of the disappearance of this border, her text *Irene is Many (Irene ist Viele)* analyses *The All Round Reduced Personality: Outtakes* (*Redupers: Die Allseitig Reduzierte Persönlichkeit*), a film by the German feminist artist Helke Sander from 1978.

Helke Sander's movie depicts the daily life of the artist Edda (performed by Sander herself) in the divided Berlin of the 1970s. The film follows the daily life of a photographer, artist, activist, single mother and member of a feminist collective, moving between various economic, social and cultural activities. During the day, Edda works as an artist and an activist, and takes care of her child and the household; at night, she photographs for a commercial Berlin newspaper and develops photos. She is also a member of an artistic collective that is in the process of organizing an exhibition on the dominating capitalist image of West Berlin. As a feminist and an independent woman, Edda has consciously decided to organize her life and work independently, in accordance with the feminist ideal of being in control of one's own life and the scheduling of one's own work. This does not mean, however, that her life is exempted from the processes of capitalist exploitation – quite the opposite.

As early as the late 1970s, Helke Sander points out a very close connection between self-organization and the new forms of capitalist work. As Marion Osten states: "What does it mean for our work and life when the social, the cultural, and the economic cease be clearly distinguishable categories and instead condition and permeate each other?"[183] It certainly means nothing good for the life of the protagonist Edda; the economic reality of self-employment, seen as emancipating to start with, seems to have a devastating effect upon her life. Edda is barely capable of fulfilling her numerous obligations; her daily life and relationships are disintegrating, she feels guilty and her working life is taking over every dimension of her being. "The emancipatory struggle that had the good life as its objective now reappears in the unsatisfied longing for change and the struggle to survive."[184]

The film depicts the hectic daily life of a visibly exhausted and ceaselessly active protagonist moving from one work assignment to the next, from one political and personal engagement to another. The self-organization of life and the establishment of an 'independent' and 'autonomous' economy reveal that these emancipating ideals are intertwined with new forms of exploitation and production, with a new understanding of engaged subjectivity. In the daily life of the artist and activist, the desire for political, feminist and cultural self-sufficiency becomes the exact opposite. The 'autonomous' and self-sufficient production does not transcend social contradictions, but embodies them to the fullest and aggravates them further, with the so-called freedom transforming into a daily dependence on numerous tasks and projects.

The embodiment of social contradictions is also characteristic of many artistic subjectivities today, where (male and female) artists switch from one activity to another; in this, the flexibility and precariousness of artistic activities goes hand in hand with the dynamic of contemporary institutions. The disappearance of the borders between art and life thus indicates the problematic social opposites in post-Fordism, where social and political work finds itself at the core of capitalist value production.

This is also the way that, from today's perspective, Lesage's essay on Ina Wudtke could be read; since the early 1990s, Wudtke has been working as an artist, activist and feminist, which makes her some kind of contemporary clone of the 'all around reduced personality' of Edda in the film by Helke Sander. The disappearance of the border between life and work in the late-capitalist work processes actually leads to the disappearance of the possibilities for an emancipating alliance between work and life, an alliance that can take place through the constant politicizing of this difference that reveals the paradoxes of contemporary autonomy, the illusory possibility of choice and self-organisation of one's life. "The entrepreneur of one's own labor should also be the artist of his/her own life."[185]

This issue is politicized in a similar way in *Expensive Darlings* (*Drage drage*, 2007), a performance by the choreographer Maja Delak. Through a choreographic exploration of the intimate and social position of the dancers, the performance highlights the problem of self-organising one's life from a feminist perspective, especially delving into the wishes, performances and arising artistic subjectivities of the protagonists. This performance, created by Delak along with other contemporary dances, needs to be viewed as a disclosure of the political and economic problems triggered by the disappearing border between life and work: the 'creative freedom' of the protagonists' lives on the edge of economic marginality results in an even greater dependence. Artistic and professional emancipation therefore does not mean the emancipation from traditional stereotypes and expectations; it does not enable a better economic status either, because the disappearance of this border is part of the contemporary exploitation of work.

If we aid ourselves with Benjamin, one of the ways of politicizing artistic work could well be a radical demand for a differentiation between work and life, between production and reproduction – i.e. a thematisation of the visibility of work as something directly connected to the methods of production. This is why it is so important to rethink the role of the artist's work and find the dividing lines between the appropriation of the value of the artist's life and life itself.

It is quite easy to succumb to the dangerous pessimism that there is nothing left that can be done, that art is fully subjugated to the capitalist forms of production and that artistic subjectivity has been completely appropriated by the capitalist way of working. The danger of this kind of pessimism does not lie so much in apathy and complaining but in hatred toward art as allegedly profoundly intertwined with capitalist interests, as without content and as elitist. This kind of hatred towards art fails to realise that its object is actually the speculative capital investment into artistic life and life in general, whereas the material and embodied artistic life actually takes place far away from such speculations.

Artists indeed mirror the contemporary work processes in their way of working, but this does not mean that they will live and work better because of it. The artist's work actually shows us that other, real side of precariousness, flexibility and the value production with life itself; life must escape the capitalist processes of exploitation. The artist's work reveals that the artist actually works at the very margin of the contemporary economy: the artist's work is at the core of value production, but is profoundly separated or entirely excluded from it. The more the pleasure of capital is projected into the artist's way of life – in other words, the more artistic life represents an obscene excess of economy – the more the artist is excluded from this economy (and thus from life).

As proof, let me just point out the numerous political changes in recent years that have directly affected the financing of the arts, educational programmes and support programmes for the arts/progressive artistic institutions at the very time when we should all actually be working as artists.[186] With this pleasure, projected into the artist's way of life (and becoming part of the capital speculations embodied in new creative residential neighbourhoods and relaxed ways of being through creative brands and heterogeneous lifestyles), the artist is losing the essence of their work: autonomy. In a way, the projection of obscene pleasure into the value of artistic life takes away the artist's public role – the antagonistic and uncapturable autonomous position connected to shaping the common by conceiving and creating new forms. As a consequence, political engagement on the part of the artist is changed into a burlesque or a fashion trend. The projection of the speculative value of artistic life shows that the formation of life is at the core of contemporary value production, because our lives are becoming our principal tasks (work). And if there is no additional value (profit) to our work any longer, we are no longer worthy of life (investment).[187]

Visible processes of work in the arts therefore become interesting when they disclose the hegemony of the difference between art and life and open up ways for representations and imagery of contemporary exploitation. In this, it is extremely important to make visible the exploitation within one's own methods of production – to work in a way that makes the production conditions visible.

Something else becomes revealed through this differentiation between life and art: the fact that the formation and creation of life is not singular, but fundamentally belongs to the common. This 'common' aspect of life was at the core of the avant-garde art reflections of the 1960s for example, when the disappearance of the difference between life and art was part of almost any artistic demand of a more radical nature. This is corroborated by some changes in recent years, especially the neoliberal measures of austerity and accusations directed towards art in terms of it not being in the public interest. Cynically, according to all the rules and regulations, artistic work should become a role model of how to work, exploit the workforce and abstract the content regardless of how problematic it may be. Quite the opposite takes place: the artist is accused of laziness and uselessness, and lives at the margin of visibility.

In more authoritarian European societies, artists also take over the role of social parasites and their activities are the first to be sanctioned. The accusing – i.e. a constant political need for the artist's work to change, which can be identified in numerous reforms of the financing and support for the arts – is a consequence of the fact that there are so many speculative desires projected into the artist's work. In other words, this work is at the core of many capitalist market fantasies: artistic work supposedly abounds in pleasure, is committed, creative, fused with life itself, committed to incessant consumption etc. We need to know that the way the artist works is not only conditioned by the economy and the market. We can also talk of aesthetic work: the reshaping and changing of perceptions, the establishing of the forms for the articulation of the common. The artist's activity is broader than the economic ideal of a 'good and successful life' or the speculative market ideals of the endless growth of value.

The aesthetic dimension of work, which is connected to the autonomy of artistic work and creating the border between life and art, connects art with the public in a special way: art has the power to conceive of the not yet conceived, to unveil conceptual contradictions and contradictions of being. I hereby understand autonomy as the establishment of the border between art and life, which profoundly determines art precisely because this difference no longer exists. This can be connected with Rancière's thoughts on the aesthetic regime of art, characterised by artistic autonomy – a notion that is still key to today's understanding of art. Within this regime, art is defined as singular and free from any specific rule or hierarchy. "Yet it does so by destroying the mimetic barrier that distinguished ways of doing and making affiliated with art from other ways of doing and making, a barrier that separated its rules from the order of social occupations. The aesthetic regime asserts the absolute singularity of art and, at the same time, destroys any pragmatic criterion for isolating this singularity"[188] When we talk about the autonomy of art, this simultaneously creates an identity of its form with the forms of life, which opens to us the entry into the understanding of the relation of art to work: "Art can show signs of being an exclusive activity insofar as it is work."[189] The autonomy of art is therefore an argument in favour of art for art's sake as opposed to the central role of work in contemporary life. This autonomy shows that aesthetic practices are not exceptional, as opposed to other practices; they are not something separate from work, but represent and reshape the division and distribution of these activities.[190] Art is and remains the common good, but in a special sense: the common good that is autonomous at the same time. Art is an autonomous fight for the articulation and forms of the public, which is currently under heavy attack due to the use of human possibilities for the production of value.

In artistic work, the visibility of work is therefore closely connected to the representation of artistic subjectivity as something that indeed constantly works, but becomes really key when this difference between life and work is radically politicised through the visibility of work. The visibility of work therefore resists the hegemonistic representation of work as something that is taking over life in its entirety. The artist's work needs to be analysed and connected to the post-Fordist way of working, as well as with the capitalist exploitation procedures in order to unveil the other, extremely important side of the artist's activity: life, which belongs to everyone, not only those who work.

5.3. The Artist's Time: Projective Temporality

In this chapter, I will discuss a form that has completely prevailed in the production of culture, as well as in the ways we economize and arrange our lives today. As discussed by Boltanski and Chiapello, the new spirit of capitalism turns work and production into an endless economic expansion and manipulation, making *the project* the basic model for productive work as well as the basic trait of life and work in general.[191] Artists, but also those working in creative professions, have a word in common that is amply used for describing what it is we do: we work on a project basis.

At first sight, 'project' seems an endlessly wide umbrella term. It is used to denote many different activities, from grand artistic events to punctured local dreams, from research activities to fishy implementations in construction work. The word seems so neutral that it becomes endlessly usable, which is also why its use does not erase the many differences that exist between individual projects. Nevertheless, the highly increased use of a notion in various social contexts and undertakings is already enough to give rise to a certain uneasiness. This uneasiness and the lightness with which the word 'project' is applied to various activities, rightfully merit being dealt with in more detail. This chapter will focus especially on the place of the project in art; the analysis of the word will attempt to shed light upon several of its characteristics that are closely connected to the changes in contemporary ways of artistic work.

Today, artists, creative workers and people who are creative in one way or another are constantly engaged in projects, often several at once, and move between the implementation of one project and the completion of another. Work exists as an endless string of projects, from starting them to finishing them at some future point; we are deeply involved in completing old projects and starting new ones. Apart from the projects set in motion, there are naturally thousands that have never been realized, those that have been conceived of for the future but never received the 'drive' for implementation, which would be the financial (or more accurately, the economic) settlement between the idea of the present and the calculation of the future. It seems that art and the creative professions have never before placed so much emphasis upon future projects (in terms of the conception, experimentation, reflection and shaping in their connection) as well as upon encouraging and practising the ability to conceive of *what is yet to happen*.

Despite the focus of creative people upon conceiving the future, we live in a time radically marked by the inability to imagine political and economic ways of life different from the known. Our times are marked by a difficulty to conceive ruptures and potential changes, which also reflects in art and in the feeling of powerlessness when we try to think about art in relation to the political. Lauren Berlant writes that the present is marked by 'cruel optimism'; we invest in those relationships and aims that actually deflate our optimism and desires; the hope for a better life depends on what prevents that hope from being realized.[192] We live in a time denoted by Stefano Harney and Valentina Desderi as one where we are frozen in the future; our attitude to the future has frozen the way in which we see work. "Under capitalism the future is an open field ahead of us that we can shape and construct through our work. Since we're condemned to have a future, we're condemned to work, and at the same time, if you are condemned to work, you are condemned to have a future. So if you want to realize your dreams you have to work (always assuming that those dreams are something that belong to a future scenario and not the present one). If you want to avoid work, you have to work as hard because you have to find a way, you have to have a plan, a strategy. Whatever you choose you will be working and you will be acting strategically, towards a goal and therefore you'll be productive. In order to change this dominant fate that wants to control the future, and therefore stay in the realm of the known, you have to sabotage this double machine of work and future so that it stops functioning for a while and that a space is opened up (a present) and later, the future will come. One way to sabotage can be to refuse strategy."[193]

Let me link my argument to *Product of Other Circumstances*, a 2010 performance by Xavier Le Roy, which intervenes into this double machine of work and future very well. The title refers to an early performance by this French choreographer, *Product of Circumstances* (1999). *Product of Circumstances* presents the autobiographic story of Xavier Le Roy, who became a choreographer after receiving a PhD in biogenetics. The performance opens up the altered ways of working in dance, expands the field of dance into other spheres of human activity and movement, and thoroughly re-evaluates the position of the choreographer's work. With *Product of Other Circumstances*, Xavier Le Roy once again finds himself in a performance that is a product of circumstances after two decades of successful artistic creation; this time however, the performance is a response to the invitation of a fellow choreographer Boris Charmatz to create a butoh performance in two weeks.[194]

In *Product of Other Circumstances*, we follow Le Roy's process of working on the performance, especially how he becomes acquainted with butoh dance, the materials he studies and how he implements them within the timeframe he has available and has agreed to. The performance can almost be read as an exhibition of the changed ways of working that have emerged in the choreographic work of today (searching for information online, the use of Wikipedia, gathering readily accessible materials). The exhibition of all this can also be understood as non-material work on contemporary performance, which profoundly changes the temporal and physical dimensions of work in dance.

The interesting thing about this performance is not so much the initial point made by Le Roy that one can become a butoh dancer in 14 days, but his accompanying statement that, due to lack of time, he created the performance in his free time – outside his professional project timetable, because it was something he has always wanted to do. But can the things artists do outside their professional time be termed art at all? Is it physically possible to work outside one's professional time? Isn't art everything that the artist does, always and everywhere?

Today, it no longer holds that everything outside one's professional time is amateurism; actually, the exact opposite might be the case: everything the artist does is amateurism, especially under the dictatorship of the accelerated time conditions of contemporary production, constant flexibility and nomadism. If the artist wishes to do what they want under the pressure of accelerated time, then it is paramount that they like their work and fully enjoy what they do not yet know, but what is destined to come. The acceleration – to learn butoh dance in two weeks – is supposed to be amateurish since butoh is a practice that requires long and painstaking work. At the same time, the acceleration of work and creation is one of the essential traits of project implementation in the fields of art and culture.

Today, the artist has no hobbies because their time is entirely devoted to art. Everything the artist does is art, but at the same time, their activity is becoming increasingly amateurish because they actually no longer have time – due to implementing projects in the future and taking care of upcoming ones; in other words, one needs to constantly maintain the connection between work and the future if one wishes to survive on the artistic market.

This intriguing connection between work and the future underlies the excessive use of the word 'project' in contemporary artistic and creative professions; it is linked with a specific time dimension of work and creation, which I will term 'projective temporality'.

The artistic processes of creation and collaboration are caught in projective temporality, with the project becoming the ultimate horizon of creation. The project is a multitude of individual works, which arise as a continuity of endless amendments because the horizon can never actually be reached or surpassed. One needs to start anew over and over, with every amendment followed by a radical break-up, i.e. the different character of another project, which is also required by the artistic market. The only people who are able to avoid this constant differing at least to some extent are the young artists, the so-called young artistic force, not interesting so much for the amendments but for the unfinished – for what is still taking shape before our eyes. For this reason, their work is rooted in residence networks, work in progress, process demonstration and open structures. The role of young artists is supposed to reveal potential values not yet identified but constantly sought after by the market. Absurdly, their actual role is often that of a cheap low-class labour force that should be held in a state of 'experimental precariousness' for as long as possible. This is why we have been able to meet so many performance artists at festivals in recent years whose 'youth' somehow just has to go on and on.

The problem with this seeming openness is that, despite its different work dynamics (i.e. using more research-oriented, open processes), it is fully subjected to the projective temporality of work. The rigid connection between work and the future does not give rise to changes in ways of being and creating, but is chiefly connected to administrating the contexts of the future and recognising future values on the artistic market. There is something destructive about projective temporality: it opens numerous possibilities, but it does not really open up the differences as well. The ultimate horizon of the work is always the completion of the project itself. The future is projected as equivalent or somehow proportionate to the present; it is presented as a continuity of the present, the future which is already foreseen as such in the project itself. The future of the project is therefore retrospective; the completion is already implemented within it.

The word 'project' must therefore be reflected on through the temporality that it implies – through the time dimension it projects. Projective temporality is the reason why artistic work and other creative industries can be analysed in close connection with capitalist production processes and why we can simultaneously observe a disappearance of a constitutive place for art in society; this disappearance is closely connected with different forms of temporality and perception. Projective temporality is also the reason for the disappearance of differences between individual projects; in the contemporary world, they usually take place through the exploitation of a flexible workforce, but still want to have a political and social impact. Projective temporality also influences the acceleration of imaginative and creative work, the furthering of transformation and new, even more radical affective individuation of the subject.

An example of the acceleration of production subjects and the omnipresent increase in projective work would be the development of the cultural-political model of independent artists or administrators/managers, which can also be viewed as a result of the political struggle for the support for non-institutional culture. Notably, it is not about the need to distinguish between artistic and organisational work, but especially about the production of subjectivity, which is at the core of this model. It is about the individualization of artistic ways and diversity, about the establishment of competitive monads that count projects in the scattered system of benefits and subsidies. The problem is that, in this kind of work, temporality is completely at the service of the implementation of the project; the relationship between work and the future is a static one, preventing other forms of collaboration, connections, persistence in time and space, and research periods that extend beyond the set evaluation periods. The unforeseeable dynamic and energy flows of creativity are standardized, the tensions and intensities are reduced and subjected to the fulfilment of the promised obligations; the affective tensions however, still focus upon the satisfaction of these obligations.

The abstraction or seeming emptiness of the word 'project' is another reason why it is necessary to rethink this notion. The word needs to be examined due to its dangerous independence and the fact that it bundles everything into the unique temporal dynamic of production: into projective temporality.

Projective temporality has numerous problematic consequences for the ways of life connected to implemented, proposed and amended projects. The project absorbs the experience of artistic work and creation, transforming this experience into a communal one as though the project was the only temporality of creation. In this, it also affects subjectivity or, more accurately, the understanding of the subjectivity involved with the completion of the project.[195] Subjectivity becomes a result of amendments; contemporary subjectivities are a sum of various projects – private, public, social and intimate. This temporality therefore affects the rhythm of the transformation of subjectivity. Subjectivity needs to be flexible, but at the same time this changing workforce, this consumption of creative energies, needs to be constantly geared towards finalisation (the completion of what is promised in the present), the realisation of the possibilities and their implementation.

A parallel comes to mind with a more topical and currently quite devastating social dimension – the role of debt in our economic, political and social relations; at the end of the day, debts are a strategy for managing the temporality of subjects. How the artistic project functions as a debt and how the guilt of indebtedness can be changed into an affirmation of one's own artistic subjectivity (albeit by taking a morally questionable opportunist stance), is demonstrated quite well in *60 Minutes of Opportunism* (2010), a performance by Ivana Müller.

The performance highlights the artist's promise to her producer that she will perform alone and live, something she has actually never done before. The value of this performance is of course linked to the value that this kind of action by a well-known artist can have for the market; the expected values are also closely connected to the choice of the artist, who must project what is still to come in proportion with the values of the future. Ivana Müller demonstrates the complexity of the choice that needs to be made by the artist, who is forever in a position of having to make opportunistic choices in order to repay the debt of expectation.

Rather than referring directly to these problems, Müller

explores this opportunist gesture in a series of performative elements that enable her to keep her promise (and repay her debt); at the same time, she reaches far beyond the border of the promise itself. She makes the work visible, but not in terms of making that a theme or placing it on the stage; she gives sense to the aesthetic structure of the performance by making the working conditions visible: what becomes visible is her initial promise that she will perform alone.

Uttered in a place in-between the interests of the market and the interests of friendship, which is frequent in artistic work, the promise (a response to a friendly invitation by the producer) calls for Müller to create a series of dramaturgic solutions in order to keep the promise but turn it upside down at the same time. She therefore has to come up with a way that enables her to perform on stage while delegating her work elsewhere. Although there is actually a lot going on, she herself just stands on the stage without moving. The activity comes from extras, recordings, images and the spectator's imagination. The pleasure of the spectator is generated by the ways in which the working conditions have been turned upside down; in other words, how intelligent humour makes it possible to cunningly avoid the conditions and promises given when working and actually not do what we initially promised.[196]

There is something else paradoxical in nature and interesting for our analysis that takes place in this way of working; it is closely linked to temporal proposals and the projection of the future still to come. In the present, *we actually run out of time*, we do not have any. It is no coincidence that our daily 'I do not have time' paradigm is so connected with the organisation of time, time management and work in the future. Projective temporality strengthens work in the future still to come while taking time away from the present – time which Henri Bergson describes as duration. The more possibilities the project opens for the future, the more time gets sucked out of the present. The present just does not seem to last. The more it is possible to project, the less time we have available for duration and persistence, for establishing, enabling and building social, political and communal relationships (which are not just spatial but mainly temporal relationships).

The intriguing relationship the project has with time has several consequences for understanding our subjectivity. As the basic production model, the project is interesting because it provides an insight into the fact that, today, the way of working includes all the areas of our lives; the project no longer knows a border between professional and personal investment – in other words, between life and work. The project not only entails work, but also self-realisation, on the level of one's life and sometimes deeply personal. The nature of this self-realisation is contradictory, however. We work so much that we never again have time for ourselves and others; due to the amount of work and the intensity of our self-realisation, we can actually burn out in life.

Interestingly, this disappearing of the present in the project and the general feeling of time loss are in contradiction to the way the project enters art in the twentieth century as a general term for artistic work. Simon Bayly's excellent essay *The End of the Project* follows the genealogy of the appearance of the word 'project' in art; one of the most interesting works presented is the study by Johnnie Gratton and Mark Sheringham on French contemporary art.[197] The two authors mention the work 'project' as a paradigm of visual culture from the beginnings of modernism, with the word especially referring to methods of working in interdisciplinary artistic practices. The use of this word can be found in performative, situational, sustainable and processual works – those foregrounding the experimental and open orientation of artistic work. The word 'project' should therefore primarily describe a processual, contingent and open practice, which cannot be planned or controlled and also entails the possibility of ending in a disaster, without a result or in something completely different and unexpected.[198]

The term 'project' began to be used in the arts as a description of highly heterogeneous practices that entail collaboration with other authors, the blurring of the boundaries between art and life, and a de-hierarchisation of ways of working. It has been part of artistic production from at least the 1960s onwards. Projects seemingly establish a new relationship with the present because their relationship with the present is experimental and considerably more playful; despite all these new forms of project-based work, projects do share a certain new attitude towards time. According to Gratton and Sheringham, the attitude to time is "rooted in the etymological and indelible make-up of the term 'project' ... temporal projection into an as yet unrealized and open future is an indispensable characteristic of anything regarded or designated as a 'project'... An 'art' of the project might suggest engagement in a process that not only takes time but offers creative ways of using, experiencing, structuring and reappropriating time, and of exploring the effects of time as change and *durée* [duration]."[199]

The present is open in terms of its relationship with what is still to come, which makes the project a contradictory temporal constellation. The project opens up the present in terms of experimentation with the present in terms of change and duration; simultaneously, this openness into the present is limited by the future – by what is not yet realised and still lies ahead. According to Bayly, the project always contains a proposition of the future, which is inseparable from the present. In my opinion, this is also where we need to search for the core of modernist approaches, despite their obsession with the present and the reduction of historical avant-gardistic utopias to the material procedures of the production of artistic work itself, this modernist approach is still inspired by the historical avant-gardes and the central utopian project of the entire twentieth century: the need to change the present. In this sense, the genealogy presented by

Gratton and Sheringham is somewhat off as the project began to become art through historical avant-gardes, with the basic objective of changing the present in the name of the future. As we know, the aim of the twentieth century was to profoundly change the world; it was forever striving for a special temporality – that of the horizon, which can never actually be reached.[200]

It is therefore essential to make a theoretical distinction between work and the project. This distinction should be understood as one of the contemporary forms of the division of labour. Today, the project is the prevailing form we work in; however it expels any present-oriented form of work. Work and the project can be differentiated through an understanding of temporality: no matter how much they may experiment with the present, all projects are projections and steps into the future, entailing a promise of the future and the possibility of what is still to come.[201] In contrast, we can understand work primarily as the preservation and maintenance of the present or a life balance that is preserved through a continuous consumption of human powers. Such understanding closely connects work with the practice of life and its consumption. It contains no other promise but that of having to maintain and preserve life. Life namely tends towards entropy, contingency and decomposure; this makes work a self-preserving aimless activity; work is the temporal activity of duration. This duration is only possible because work is the way of the community; its collective and community-based character has already been discussed by Marx.[202] Work is not just an inevitable human relationship with nature or a passively shared state; it places us into a relationship with other people: "to work is to work in relation to others."[203]

Common work is also a paradoxical work without properties, which makes it similar to autonomous work, discussed by André Gorz. Gorz places work without properties in opposition with productive work; common work is not 'collective work' or operative work with a common goal, but something that places us into a relationship because it does not have any aims or properties – its essence is that of preserving life in an anarchic manner.[204]

In a short essay, Boyan Manchev elaborates on Gorz's understanding of life without properties, linking it with a special kind of temporality – that of the time of performance which is in contrast with performance time. In doing so, Manchev wishes to demonstrate a bizarre shift in the understanding of contemporary work, which springs from "the perverse understanding of artistic work as a sort of a leisure experience, with no sign of constraint, exploitation, physical effort, sensible experience of matter."[205] The future-related promises constantly deceive us that everything we do in a project is a leisurely experience in which we experiment with our lives and sociality for a promise in the future. The project therefore belongs to the exploitation of common work, to the commodification of the common, where sociability itself is in the core of exploitation.

For this reason, many experimental and performative artistic practices of the 1960s and 1970s (e.g. Allan Kaprow, group OHO, the time paintings by Roman Opalka, neoavant-garde theatres) explored the current production procedures and opened up artistic work to work procedures. This was a kind of rebellion against the future dimension; at the same time, these practices have an interesting relationship to the future – they entail a constant emancipatory moment that commits art to what is still to come and again opens art to the project. The reflection on artistic work and the ways in which production procedures enter and become visible within artistic work can also clearly reveal the true nature of capitalised work, which becomes increasingly similar to artistic work today. We can even claim that, through its rebellion against capitalisation (of time, energies, language, forms), art radically attempts to commit to the present procedures of production and consumption while creative, cognitive and post-Fordist work takes over the utopian, future-oriented and speculative nature of art. The aforementioned type of work is committed to the creation of the future, to changes and to the revolutionisation of ways of working, and to the furthering of creativity. Such capitalised projects are bound to actualise their speculative excess, including at the expense of killing the present. In this sense, many artworks of the 1960s place the visibility of work at the forefront; in the attempt to somehow distance themselves from the exploitation of human abilities, they focus upon production (of the body, materials, temporality, space). This exploitation is also deeply ingrained in the production of art, especially through the investment of phantasms into the artist's life, as discussed in the previous chapter.[206]

Numerous artistic practices emerged as unpredictable sums of coincidences, maintained material identities, duration etc. can be read from the perspective of insistence on the preservation of the presence of work. We could even say that contemporary production can be considerably better analysed not so much in terms of the division between material and non-material work (lately, this division has even been criticised by its advocates)[207], but in terms of the temporality of work and the differences that this temporality establishes between work and the project.

With the aid of Henri Lefebvre, Simon Bayly deals with the difference between continuous everyday work and project work, the aim of which is always to change the existing state of things: "what might be a project for, say, the new museum's architect, is merely a temporary work place for the electrician wiring the fire alarm system."[208] According to Bayly, this difference helps us understand that 'life in a project' is actually a subjective and existential state, but that it is today becoming a problematic prevailing and universal tendency in the understanding of contemporary work and production. This 'life in a project' also helps us understand the speculative investment of contemporary capital into the life of the artist, where the artist's work is viewed as an incessant changing of the present, a progressive actualisation of life potentialities and a glance into the future that takes place through numerous self-evaluations and proposals yet to come. This speculative life is far from the preservation and daily material process of life balance; it is also radically divorced from embodied differences and space singularities, which is why numerous projects often seem the same.

The acceleration of projects and the activities of their new beginning and implementation thus make it possible for change to occur only at the moment of crisis, exhaustion or retreat. This kind of movement towards the completion and consummation of the proposal is problematic because we do not actually talk about chronological temporality (where one thing follows another), about the narrative (utopian, dystopian etc.) or of progress, but rather of the balance between the future and the present that projects what is still to come: the project is therefore closer to messianic temporality. This kind of balance, which actually 'freezes' time into a multitude of amendments, has destructive consequences for subjectivity and the communities within which artistic proposals are created. The artist is increasingly distant from work contexts, which do not seem to have any major differences between their particular articulations. Differences between creative communities become invisible, disabling their political power, which is always based on the singularity of the artistic gesture.

The project therefore becomes the ultimate horizon of experience and it is not unusual that another frequently used word in cultural and creative production also refers to the dynamic of this temporality: the word I have in mind, of course, is *deadline*. At the end of the project, there is this 'line of death'; it is a moment of pure fulfilment, the final consumption of creative life without an experience that would follow it. To put it another way: the project is a promise in the future, but it can only be realised as a catastrophe; one namely needs to cross the line of death in order to be able to implement the project. This tension is somewhat alleviated by the fact that life goes on regardless of that line because so many other projects remain to be finished; in this way, the horizon only moves away a little when we wish to touch it. In this way, the future is radically closed in its endless possibilities, and the possibility of experimenting with the present is disabled.

In project temporality, the possibility of the future is actually in balance with the current power relations. These current power relations give us the illusion that it is possible to predict the unpredictable; the future therefore seems increasingly calculated. In this sense, project temporality is not directly connected to the time structure of debt. The time structure of debt is also discussed by Lazzarato; he states that it is no coincidence that debt has traditionally been considered as stealing time. The system of debt must neutralise time; it is necessary to prevent any kind of potentially deviant behaviour on the part of the debtor. The economy of debt is therefore the economy of time and subjectivization in a very special way; the balance with the future can only achieved in balance with what already exists.[209]

The temporality of the project is therefore contradictory. The project works as a fatal openness, full of libidinal possibilities of what is still to come but, at the same time, including the line of death. The project can therefore be analysed as *eros* and *thanatos* together. It is this catastrophic dimension, the incessant exhaustion of life forces and the closeness of death that also mark today's affective feeling of work, which consequently arises from the exploiting of the human powers and potentials.[210] In project work, the future dimension of work is catastrophic; every attempt to change the present in relation to the future brings calamity and disaster and is inevitably connected to failure. The projective attitude to the present is marked by risk and uncertainty; this argument is quite in line with Lefebvre's thinking about work: "No matter how close it gets to success, every endeavour is destined to fail in the end... Every totalisation which aspires to achieve totality collapses, but only after it has been explicit about what it considers its inherent virtualities to be. When it makes the illusory, outrageous, and self-totalizing claim that it is a world on the human (and thus finite) scale, the negative (limitation, finiteness) that this 'world' has always borne within itself begins eating it away, refuting it, dismantling it, and finally brings it tumbling down. Only when a totality has been achieved does it become apparent that it is not a totality at all."[211]

Today, we work incessantly in order to open up the future through work; we experiment with our own lives and the lives of others. The more we work the stronger our feeling that we do not control work but that work controls us. Project work is therefore connected to a constant catastrophic feeling that, as a totality with which we are supposed to redo our lives (and our present), work is on the verge of collapse. Interestingly, this prevailing way of working gives a feeling (even in the case of the smallest of projects) that it transforms the whole world or at least life in general; in this manner, it even more radically influences the acceleration of duration and present time, establishing a specifically 'economizing' attitude toward life – we work responsibly for the future while the present slips continously through our fingers.

At the end of this chapter, I would once again like to point out the opposition between how *the project actually enters into the work of art* and *the project as the prevailing mode of production of artistic work*. The project enters art as a naming for open, processual and interdisciplinary artistic practices that are supposed to focus on the material processes of the present – on the inherent temporality of the duration of life that is disappearing from today's project work. Project work is therefore a means through which art is supposed to come close to life and open itself to the heterogeneous processes of life, which are in turn open towards the future that is yet to come. As Boris Groys points out in his essay *The Loneliness of the Project*, the project is always committed to parallel temporality of or the temporal exclusion from the daily flow of life. The project is actually a temporary and sometimes also a permanent retreat from life (characteristic e.g. of religious communities as well as artistic projects). The project is therefore marked by desynchronised time; when working on a project, we are actually separated from the time as experienced by society and the community. "But somewhere beyond this general flow of time, someone has begun working on a project–writing a book, preparing an exhibition, or plotting a spectacular assassination–in the hopes that the completed project will alter the general run of things and all mankind will be bequeathed a different future: the very future, in fact, anticipated and aspired to in this project."[212]

Groys characterizes the creation of the project as "socially sanctioned loneliness"[213], desynchronised with the flow of time but required to offer something in return when it comes to an end. The loneliness discussed by Groys brings up a paradoxical image of the modern solipsist artist, a loner, potentially an "idiot"[214], who temporarily leaves society due to the need for a change in the life he or she is a part of. The project is capable of taking itself out of the flow of life because it is based on the hope that it will again be able to harmonise with social reality at a later point.

This temporal harmonisation is contradictory in character because it is possible only due to the change that the project is supposed to bring. For this reason, this harmonisation is always a harmonisation of something different, of something that has already taken itself out of society (regardless of whether the project is successful or not). Many loners can be found in performance art pieces and experimental events involving the audience, in which art came close to life by actually stepping out of it: it creates special conditions of experience (hence the emphasis on rules, scores, scripts, etc.) which could induce change in the method of perception and the creation of aesthetic forms.[215] Loners can also be found earlier, e.g. in the projects of the historical avant-garde – the first 'projects in art' proper, committed to a universal change of human life if not that of the universe.

Groys points out the problematic character of such historical avant-garde endeavours committed to utopian universal projects with the aim of shaping a new future for everyone, but by means of hermetic language and forms that could only be communicated in self-isolation. This also makes the project a modern phenomenon whose implementation is based on exclusion and exclusivity, which gives a highly contradictory status to modernity and its yearning for progress. As Groys states, the problem is that the resynchronisation with society – the aim of every successful or unsuccessful project – entails a feeling of sickness: what gets lost is the feeling of being suspended in parallel time, of belonging to excluded life "beyond the general run of things".[216] Today, this kind of socially sanctioned loneliness characterises work of any kind whatsoever. We frequently work as loners, preparing one project after another while being solipsistically isolated from the communal practice of daily life. The basic symptom of this isolation is the sense of a general lack of time. This state could also be described as a contradiction of modern existence. Jason Read terms modern existence 'social isolation', springing from the contemporary simultaneous exploitation of human communicative and social potentiality, the contemporary alienation of our sociality, in which social bonds become subject to private choice and market offer while our common essence is at the core of exploitation.[217]

Let me refer to another artistic work at this point. It can tell us a lot about the interesting symptoms of this difficult illness, the resynchronisation with life that is required in numerous contemporary artistic projects. At the beginning of his documentary video *Documentation of Selected Works 1971 – 1975*, the artist Chris Burden spends about ten minutes talking about the works that we are about to see in the film. A considerable part of this introduction (in which Burden talks in close-up, so that we are only able to see his face), focuses on how we are to watch the footage, during which we need be aware throughout that these were true events, but that what we are about to see is far from what actually happened: "I want you to ... try to remain aware that you're not seeing the actual experience."[218]

If read in the light of our reflection on the project, Burden's address is not only interesting as a defence of the 'authentic feeling' of the live event, which cannot be captured on film, but also as an argument for this special and temporally unique social situation of the artist and the participants in the event desynchronised with reality. It is a defence of this special illness of exclusion from the order of things, which is discussed by Groys and necessarily remains after the end of the project, a defence of the idiotic loneliness that comes to a definite end when the event becomes part of social reality.

Burden's address is especially interesting because this is an early documentation of artistic works in the field of performance art, where the division between work and documentation is still naively obvious as far as their status and understanding of reality are concerned. Burden strictly differentiates between the event and its documentation; the project is therefore still on the side of the event. As stated by Groys, documentation in contemporary art should be considered in close connection with the project (and, may I add, ultimately makes even the most idiotic attempts not seem idiotic). Today, the document is the basic witness to the artistic project, to the successful or unsuccessful synchronisation with reality. The artistic project cannot be evaluated as a result – in other words, we can never say with certainty whether the aim has been met or not (i.e. whether the project has achieved what it was supposed to). "Our attention is thereby shifted away from the production of a work (including a work of art) onto life in the art project–a life that is not primarily a productive process that is not tailored to developing a product, that is not "result-oriented." Under these terms, art is no longer understood as the production of works of art but as documentation of life-in-the-project–regardless of the outcome. This clearly has an effect on the way art is now defined, as art no longer manifests as another, new object for contemplation produced by the artist, but as another, heterogeneous timeframe of the art project, which is documented as such."[219]

In contemporary artistic institutions, we actually do not witness artistic works, but the production and documentation of life as a pure activity by means of art. According to Groys, art has become bio-political in this sense; we are again confronted with the relationship between art and life, but in a totally different constellation. This relationship is "characterized by the paradox of art in the guise of the art project, now also wanting to become life, instead of, say, simply reproducing life or furnishing it with art objects."[220]

What we actually witness in numerous contemporary artistic institutions are documented processes, artistic procedures and documented states of exclusion from the everyday order of things. In my opinion, this exclusion is also the reason for the popularity of performative events in visual art in recent years; this particularity gives rise to the feeling that there has actually been a change in the present, that something has finally happened. The feeling of enlivenment in contemporary artistic institutions is frequently a part of isolated and socially sanctioned loneliness (in which we can finally break its norms).

On the one hand, project work, prevalent in contemporary culture, actually exhausts the present because this kind of work entails life itself. On the other hand, work as a material process (practice itself) remains without value because such work cannot be isolated and included in the conception of the future. It is always subject to the flow of unforeseeable time and common relationships as well as to the entropy of work's further attempts and repetitions.

Groys uses the project to talk about the change in the understanding of art. However, we could also connect the project with wider changes in the field of the exploitation of human powers and creativity; human powers and creativity need to be constantly arranged and evaluated like many other projects. An interesting part of this exploitation is the fact that the project actually delegates the singular gesture of the one who works, that it actually shifts the authorship and creative gesture of the artist elsewhere.

When making projects, we no longer work as authors, but delegate our authorship to a multitude of evaluative, managerial and organisational processes that projective temporality needs to be constantly subordinated to. Furthermore, we can no longer talk about the function of the author because the commonality of creativity and the discursive network of various proposals are at the centre of production. The project should be research-oriented, should contain an individual investment, and should subordinate life to itself for the duration of its implementation. It ultimately turns out that its authorisation no longer depends on our or common creative gesture and investment.

The following questions, also faced by many project proposers, is therefore extremely interesting: who authorizes the project, i.e. how do you establish whether the project has been successful or not, and how do you approve the financing of a project and according to what criteria? The exhaustion arising from project work springs from the fact that the legitimacy of the project is not in its actual implementation and the implementer, but belongs to a higher anonymous bureaucratic and managerial authority, the structural power. Those investing themselves entirely into the project, actually delegate their life powers to another authority. Such is also the functioning of today's bio-political power, which can fully reject life regardless of its implementation.

Project work accelerates time and intensifies exhaustion because nobody is the author of their project anymore despite their considerable investment into it. As Simon Bayly states, those working on a project are only project agents. In their project proposal and implementation, they need to constantly reply to and correspond with the systems of power, evaluations and intermediation of the intermediators responsible for the evaluation and speculative comparison of value.[221] According to this scenario, whose agents we have become, it is also constantly expected that we especially perform our own selves, i.e. that we ceaselessly perform ourselves as working subjects and creative beings of the contemporary world.

This brings us back to art and Groys's thesis on the documentation of art that has become life. Maybe this is why art has the power to open up the aesthetic dimension of the process of life, work and activity as such. The power of art ultimately does not arise from the management systems, but from the temporal contingency and entropy of its material practice. So if it wishes to survive at work, art needs to rebel against the project and demand the temporality of work as duration.

Conclusion

On Laziness and less Work

The aim of this book is to draw on the relationship between art and work, as well as on reflections on the characteristics of artistic labour, in order to show how art approaches capitalism and at the same time resists the capitalist appropriation of human power and creation. The contemporary relationship between art and work is closely connected to the relationship between work and life as well as with the ways that life (subjectivity, sociality, temporality, movement) has been entering the core of contemporary production. My argument is based on the belief that art is a way of life, but not in the sense that the border between life and art is disappearing; in fact, this border establishes itself time and time again, creating forms and representations of life as well as shaping the language of art. Art is a form of life, its perceptive and aesthetic power, the life yet to come. These ways radically change the conditions of common life, the intensity of co-being and the existing forms of subjectivisation. Art could therefore be connected to the disclosure and shaping of life conditions as well as with perceptive, affective and presentational proposals. Such proposals can profoundly shatter the conditions of art itself, as they are articulated regardless of existing power relations. Today, the relationship between art and life is highly topical because their merger underlies the capitalisation of human powers and their exploitation for the generation of profit. In contemporary ways of working, the boundary between production and reproduction is disappearing. In this, art is of central importance; it comes across as the ideal and most speculative representation of this disappearance, which is why it is at the very centre of the capitalist interest in generating value. It is therefore essential to critically analyse the labour of the artist and connect it to the post-Fordist way of working, as well as with capitalist exploitation procedures.

This kind of understanding of art is especially important at a time that often feels one of crisis and transformation – a time of an excess prevalence of capitalism on the one hand and the radical powerlessness of political activity and the inability to think the future on the other. Interestingly, after two decades of 'political art' and constant transgression of the border between life and art, the art of today faces a deep crisis in terms of value articulation and its social role; at the same time, it is under attack from rightist politics in connection with the neoliberal understanding of freedom.

Although we have been confronted with numerous engaged, political and critical artistic projects over the last two decades, their pseudo-activity makes them ineffective and they fail to penetrate and affect the social field. The pseudo-engagement of art has also contributed to making art a target of dangerous populist reproaches that art is but 'leftist elitism'; in this, it is claimed that art is an activity that does not interest the public and has no social role or influence, whereby the artists enjoy subsidies from the state and their alleged 'laziness' is protected from the self-regulating and dynamic nature of the market.

Although there are several 'classic' arguments in this tirade that come up fairly constantly as a part of a completely erroneous moral belief (that artists supposedly do not work), these need to be looked at more closely. It is important to recognize that the arguments against the elitism of contemporary art belong to a fusion of populist and neoliberal rhetoric with the aim of profoundly revaluating the articulation of the common and the community in contemporary society. In this populist and corporate language, the community and the common are left to the decisions of 'free' individuals in the market; these people will choose (buy) whatever they like or whatever suits them most, and thus shape their relationships and connections with others in accordance with their own individual desires (interestingly, the belief in the *a priori* rationality of choice is never questioned in this instance).²²² Along these lines, art is a result of the choices made by individuals rather than for the common good; and beyond even this, in the light of populist rhetoric, any support for and cultivation of the common good is viewed as political elitism, an engaged leftist circle.²²³ There are many layers to this problem. On the one hand, this populist argument against art requires a revaluation of the notion of the public, and on the other it touches upon the core of the problematic politicisation of art over the last two decades. It is a fact that, although the art of this period has never ceased to be interested in political activity, it has simultaneously become distanced from the political public sphere.

In the conclusion of the book, I would like to discuss three different lines of argument that should indicate the possibilities of an affirmation of art and its public place today. I would like to show that these arguments need to be disobediently rethought so that the artist's work can withstand the exploitation of creative power and, at the same time, reveal itself as a potentiality of the common – so that the work of the artist may be open to the lives of everyone, not only to those who work.

I.

The first disobedience concerns the relationship between art and the economy — the 'economic' argument for the usefulness of art that goes something like this: it is bad not to support art because art also produces economic value.²²⁴ This therefore concerns argumentation about the value of art, which goes hand in hand with the value of artistic work (both in the sense of works created by artists and works performed by them). Many active participants in the arts nowadays, who fight political pressure and radical financial cuts to subsidies and support for the arts on various fronts, articulate common interest as economic value; oftentimes, part of the arguments in favour of the arts is the fact that they form an important part of the contemporary economy and the creative industries, generating important economic value.

Although it is sometimes wise to use the language of one's opponent in political argumentation, this argument is actually false and does not affirm the value of artistic activity as such: the arts do not have an economic value because one cannot speculate on the value of what is to come. The proposals for common being, which are articulated regardless of the existing power relations, can never be evaluated. If art really needs to be affirmed through the language of economics, it needs to be pointed out that art is not connected to the economy of the production of value but is much closer to aimless spending, to giving gifts without expecting a return. This is discussed by Robert Pfaller, who argues that the basic trait of the economy of art is actually lavish consumption.[225] Pfaller states that this understanding is closer to Bataille's notion of consumption and points out something important when we think about the relationship between art and economics. It is not only that art spends senselessly; an enormous part of consumption is senseless in the contemporary capitalist economy as well, but the difference is that the senseless consumption in the arts is constantly visible: the fact that we openly embark on lavish senseless spending (and without any repayment at that) is the very power of art.

According to Bataille, every society will generate surplus; the surplus will be spent or wasted, but societies differ in *the way* this is done.[226] "Therein lies the greatest difference compared to the present day. Today, we spend without noticing. Our consumption exists, but not on a grand scale abounding with pleasure. This is why today's society destroys its surpluses through forms of unconscious pleasure that are actually neurotic and devoid of pleasure."[227] The economy of invisible spending places its impediments everywhere; according to Pfaller, this is also the case in the arts: "In this field, there are the impediments and consumption mechanisms of curating and intermediation, so that there are at least two curators and agents per artist nowadays. The rest of today's artists are hardly productive at all: within an artist's work, actual artistic work only has a decreasing 10 per cent share in comparison to studying the market, self-marketing, public relations, branding, socializing etc."[228]

Therefore, the production of life and sociality are at the core of the ways of working in the arts; these are the ways in which creative powers are capitalized and also in which impediments are placed upon their consumption and spending. One could claim something similar for other creative fields like science and education, which are also under the considerable pressure of economization and rationalization.[229] It is no good to moralize over this kind of intermediation (in terms of art being destroyed by the various intermediators); it needs to be noted that constant spending and lavishing takes place in the intermediation and the economization of the arts – in the production and market models of the arts. At the same time, this intermediation functions as an impediment to lavishness; it attempts to make this spending 'meaningful', to control the affective atmospheres and forces of spending. This also has a lot to do with the instability of value, which must be rendered rational and transparent, at least in appearance. "Just as there are societies that know they make magic and those that are not aware of that, there are societies that know they spend and those that are not aware of it. It is the latter that have created huge spending mechanisms that gobble up their sources. Since they are not aware of it, they also miss out on the magical glow, the glamour of their spending, and thus no longer know the feeling of doing things on a grand scale."[230]

The contradiction of contemporary consumption can also be viewed along these lines: with today's irrational, neurotic spending and a lavishness that radically alters and destroys nature, this consumption is utterly neurotic and destructive to life. In view of this, Pfaller claims, "Bataille's objection to the advocates of efficiency would be entirely different. Bataille would not say: do give us some money so that the human side will not be completely extinguished in the process. But he would also not say: look, we can also be efficient from time to time and demonstrate the still invisible practicability of our undertakings."[231]

When defending the 'economic effects' of art, the answer to the question of why art needs to be defended in the first place should be based neither on the metaphysical 'humanist' argument nor on pragmatic arguments in terms of its efficiency and economic profitability. Lavish consumption resists the interpretation of art as something that defends the human essence in this time of raging capitalism, but also refuses to agree with the contemporary economic understanding of art as a part of the creative industries. These two interpretations are most frequent when art finds itself in the grip of financial strictness and under critical attacks. Public discussions attempt to shed light on the hidden essence of art (art civilizes, does something good etc.) or stress its usefulness (art gives rise to profit and value). According to Pfaller though, Bataille's response to the critical reproaches would be entirely different: "Let us talk openly. We have clearly not co-operated enough so far. This gives you a reason to limit us by means of various consumption mechanisms. However, as a test, simply give us the funds you now use for spin doctors, evaluation gendarmes, reform preachers, education agencies etc. and you will see: we will certainly use these sources down to the last cent, for cultural and cultural-theoretical expenses abounding in pleasure. Unlike now, we and you will be surrounded by the beautiful glamour of doing things on a grand scale."[232]

This beautiful glamour is not only an aesthetic category but also the category of common pleasure arising from consumption. The affirming of art with the language of economics is therefore yet another false consequence of the 'political' pseudo-activity of art; a time might be coming when the most radical politicisation of art will be its detachment from any kind of economic value in order to reveal new affective and aesthetic articulations of the community. Art deals with social problems and it is constantly pseudo-active because we live in a time with a radical inability to establish and conceive of a reality through which people's communities could be articulated. We live in a time of the disappearance and rearticulating of the public, the disappearance of the public sphere. If, therefore, we wish actually to speak of political art, we need to discuss its relationship with the common.

Along the same lines, we also need to rethink the social and political values of art, which are connected to the perception, recognition and establishment of the various forms of visibility of what we have and will have in common. At the same time, art is also closely connected to the new politics of temporality, which no longer participate in the endless production of the new, and in training for the creative contexts with which it will be possible to prevail in the contemporary market of provocative and political artistic projects. In this sense, art has a lot to do with 'doing things on a grand scale', as Pfaller argues; this refers to the pleasure of life and creation when spending and creating, the pleasure felt when creating and gifting senselessly, in the endless lavishness and creation of a life in common.

II.

The second line of argument for disobedience concerns the artist's relation to work, especially the usefulness and productive nature of that work, which affects every dimension of an artist's life (and therefore also comes across as a fusion of life and work). Not only is this a time when numerous kinds of work and activities (not only artistic) are becoming 'useless' and unnecessary, it is also a time when one's potential abilities must be constantly updated: one needs to constantly perform oneself in a way that allows one to become something other than one already is.

Contemporary work is strongly marked by transformation and flexibility; this does not actually open up new possibilities though, but frequently results in even more rigid and exploitative working conditions, in which every moment (including those of inactivity) is dedicated to seizing work better. Many artistic practices and ways of working should therefore be viewed as a resistance to this kind of definition of all activities through human work; for this reason, many contemporary artistic works are interested in methods of creation that have an interesting and incestuous relationship with laziness and non-work: mistakes, minimum effort, coincidence, duration, passivity, etc. This intertwining between work and non-work, or between activity and laziness, is also connected to what I discussed earlier: visible senseless spending. It reveals the materiality of work, which is closely connected to time and space and is no longer considered project-type headway towards the goal, but can also embrace long periods of passivity, sleep, inactivity etc.

In a photography series with the telling title of *Artist at Work*, the Croatian conceptual artist Mladen Stilinović is depicted in his sleep in his bed, covered with a blanket and in various sleeping positions. In 1992, the same author published the text *In Praise of Laziness*, inspired by *Laziness as the Truth of Mankind* (1921) by Kamizir Malevich, in which he claims that laziness is the mother of life. In his writing, Malevich condemns socialism's obsession with work and is also critical towards capitalism, which enables laziness for a select few. *In Praise of Laziness* continues this comparison of the different concepts of laziness in Eastern and Western Europe (the socialist and capitalist worlds).

At the beginning of the 1990s, Stilinović offers an interesting interpretation and one that, in my opinion, is highly topical for the present time. He points out an interesting difference between artists from the West (Europe and the US) and the East (the former Eastern European countries): "As an artist, I learned from both East (socialism) and West (capitalism). Of course, now when the borders and political systems have changed, such an experience will be no longer possible. But what I have learned from that dialogue, stays with me. My observation and knowledge of Western art has lately led me to a conclusion that art cannot exist... any more in the West. This is not to say that there isn't any. Why cannot art exist anymore in the West? The answer is simple. Artists in the West are not lazy. Artists from the East are lazy; whether they will stay lazy now when they are no longer Eastern artists, remains to be seen."[233] In this way, Stilinović's manifesto touches upon yet another kind of wasteful consumption – laziness, which often wastes the most precious commodity of life in the present day, i.e. time.

After two decades have passed since the creation of Stilinović's text, we can say that artists from the 'East' are no longer lazy either but participate in the methods of western artistic production, with the last traces of laziness having been successfully expelled by the transition processes. I therefore read Stilinović's text as an insightful and humorous analysis of a certain situation that reveals many aspects of the close connection between art and capitalism, which was especially visible to artists from the East at the beginning of the nineties, because the history of their practices was characterized by a different attitude to work. In comparison with socialism, capitalism has always been characterized by the artistic system (a developed system of contemporary art institutions, the market mechanisms of the presentation of contemporary art etc.) – a system that developed contemporary art and was not known in socialist countries. But this is not about contemporary art not having existed in the East; it did, however it developed under different circumstances.

There was an absence of what Stilinović ironically describes as the preoccupation of the artists from the West with irrelevant things "such as production, promotion, the gallery system, the museum system, the competition system (who is first), their preoccupation with objects, all that drives them away from laziness, away from art. Just as money is paper, so a gallery is a room"[234]. The artists of the East were therefore "lazy and poor because the entire system of insignificant factors did not exist. Therefore they had time enough to concentrate on art and laziness. Even when they did produce art, they knew it was in vain, it was nothing".

The difference between the East and the West is thus reduced to a thought hypothesis that tries to affirm the creation of art in the East with the absence of the capitalist system of the production and dissemination of art. The contradictory nature of the hypothesis is deliberate, as it is generally believed that the development of art in the East was not similar to that in the West due to the absence of this system (contemporary art institutions and the artistic market). For this reason, 'Eastern' art is practically non-existent in the canonized collections of contemporary art; also, the history of contemporary art of the East is still more or less invisible.[235]

At the same time though, it is true that the East formed other models for making and producing art as well as other methods of collaboration and connection between artists that were not part of institutional forms similar to those in the West.[236] Although the prevailing opinion at the beginning of the 1990s was that the art of the East remained somewhat invisible and marginalized because it had not developed its institutions, this lack could also be reflected on from an affirmative standpoint: it could be rethought what this subversive affirmation of 'the absence of production models' actually brings. This is what Stilinović does in his manifesto; his artistic work points out the problematic connection between art and work. Work is actually at the forefront in both communist and capitalist societies; work is believed to be the way one finds one's purpose and becomes a part of society. In a communist society the artist is still able to question this centrality of work, disclose its hypocritical ideological matrix and point out the true layabouts at the centre of the ideology of work.

This is also what Stilinović does in a number of his works from the 1970s and 1980s that demonstrate the paradoxes of celebrating work through rest, for example in his series of works dedicated to the 1st of May (Labour Day) or by depicting the artist as a layabout (the photographic series *Artist at Work*). Today this disclosure of the non-work at the centre of work seems to have become impossible because today's artists are always primarily focused on working; even artists can only be lazy in order to work better. In this, the central value of work, the constant changes to the different kinds of professional expertise, flexibility and the close connection between work and the manner of production are rarely questioned.

As I attempted to show in the book, the actual problem is that communication, creativity and potentiality of subjectivity are at the very core of artistic work. In terms of the manner of working, the contemporary worker is close to what the artist should be doing; the contemporary ways of working and artistic pursuits seem to have nearly fused. At the same time, there is a modality to contemporary work that, despite all the freedom this work offers, does not allow for futile activities; as Stilinović writes, the artist of today cannot work with an awareness that what he/she does is actually nothing. Or, if we come back to Pfaller, an awareness that the activity of the artist is actually visible and lavish senseless consumption. Quite the opposite: a part of artistic work is the numerous conceptualizations and determinations created by the mediators, in the sense that the artist's work is hardly nothing and empty spending.

Useless as it may be, every activity must have a purpose and strive for a value on the market; every futile activity needs to be shown to have value. Stilinović's text from the beginning of the 1990s points out several key changes in artistic work, or in the ways artists perform their work; at the forefront, there are the centrality of work, the artist as an entrepreneurial person, constant nomadism, the constant readiness to reflect upon one's work, participation in the presentation and dissemination of one's own production, the networking aspect of work, and the internationalization of work. In this, the artist actually does not have the time or scope for other types of creativity, those also connected to other temporal modalities of being. At the same time, Stilinović's manifesto can also be read as a process of affirming the methods of artistic creation that have emerged outside the capitalist art systems, or at least as a manifest way of stepping on the brake, as an attempt to elude the temporal totality of capitalism that connects the acceleration of contemporary time with the visibility of work.

There is something else that needs to be added to Stilinović's manifesto. It is the massive amount of work performed by the artist that makes him or her lose the political power to show or expose the true layabouts at the core of the capitalist ideology of work. The lazy artist of socialism was still able to hold up a mirror of irony to the ideological hypocrisy of the celebration of work; with the absence of institutions that could provide work, the artist actually needed to remain without work if he or she wanted to remain an artist. Today, the artist cannot remain without work if he or she wants to remain an artist; this is why the artist works constantly and, at the same time, must be incessantly critical of their work. Their every gesture, no matter how lazy it may be, must necessarily be turned into work – if not by the artist themselves, then in connection with the institutions and other elements of the system that make the artist's work visible and evaluate it as work.

In this constant striving to expel any trace of laziness from his or her useless work, the artist overlooks the fact that this is how he or she loses any critical power to hold up a mirror to the true layabouts at the core of the capitalist system. According to the philosopher Aaron Schuster, the problem is that laziness was finally subdued by neoliberalism, yet can actually be found at the neoliberal core. "Contrary to protestant work ethics, postmodern work ethics are basically some kind of tolerated guided laziness. The enigmatic and tragic character of Bartleby has changed into a universal farce, into the absurdity of contemporary corporate life".[237] According to Schuster, this is why some of the laziest masters of this planet are the credit rating agencies, companies that affect the fate of the entire planet by 'opinions only' and without any public accountability whatsoever.

While laziness is the new postmodern ethic cultivated by those who speculate and evaluate the future, the artist works incessantly, producing critical models, reflecting, warning, problematizing, provoking and participating publicly in one way or another. The most absurd thing is that the artist is still frequently considered a parasite and a free-thinking freeloader who needs public funding instead of establishing themselves on the 'free' market. In my opinion, these reproaches need to be connected to the spread of laziness at the core of capitalism, whose speculations and creative solutions can only spread by simultaneously erasing the antagonistic sphere of the public – everything that belongs to and is valued as the common good. It is in this public sphere where the artist needs to be active.

Even though the closeness of art and capitalism calls many practices into question, art still plays a very important role in the constitution of the social. After all, this always becomes apparent at the moment the public field has been put under a question mark: every intervention into the privatization of the public and every attempt to exploit the public sphere always highlight the issue of art. The attempt to leave art to private interests is therefore equivalent to striving for everyone to work for their own private interest and in this way, indeed, to become rich layabouts. As Schuster writes, the problem is that this easy life always slips away and the necessity of working remains.

III.

As Hannah Arendt writes in her book *The Human Condition*, all activities in the public sphere have become labour. This has resulted in the fact that everything we do is pushed to the lowest level of supplying life's necessities and sufficient living standards.[238] 'Making a living' thus becomes the centre of contemporary life. The consequence of the liberation of work is not only the entry of workers into the public sphere; without doubt, work also rules everything else. In this sense, the prevalence of work is by no means connected to freedom and emancipation but to the omnipresent yoke of necessity.

At the same time, the utopian liberation from work (also demanded by Marx) is not a proper answer to the prevalence of work, because work is closely connected to the materiality of life and the painstaking preservation of nature. According to Arendt, this working life would never be human life proper if "man-made world of things, the human artifice erected by *homo faber*, becomes a home for mortal men, whose stability will endure and outlast the ever-changing movement of their lives and actions, only insomuch as it transcends both the sheer functionalism of things produced for consumption and the sheer utility of objects produced for use."[239] According to Arendt, the only exception that society is still willing to grant is that of the artistic professions: "the artist, who, strictly speaking, is the only 'worker' left in a labouring society".[240]

I deal with the changes in artistic ways of working in order to show that, today, the 'artistic profession' is no longer so 'exceptional' because the place of art in society has undergone profound changes in the last few decades. Subordinated to the necessity of work, artistic work no longer knows a division between life and work: every aspect of life is an aspect of labour. It is flexible and subordinated to the project-oriented logic of work. It is losing its autonomy and is regulated by numerous mechanisms of evaluation. Furthermore, the situation of artistic work is even more complex than that.

Although artistic work is no longer exceptional because it is subordinated to the necessity of work (i.e., it is more and more about working and less and less about creating), it does preserve its exceptional place within the capital and economic speculations on artistic life, which is ascribed social and economic value as a kind of life that is actually free from work; in bizarre contemporary phantasms on creativity, it turns into 'pure creation'. Artistic work is therefore at the core of the twisted ideological relationship between work and freedom; cynically, the work that comes across as the freest is the work that is completely fused with life. The work considered free is the kind whose level of dedication and intensity leaves no further room for life. According to Arendt, work as liberation from work can be described as a highly intense life process,[241] and contemporary work actually seems precisely that: a highly intense life that often has a devastating effect on the subjects who invest into it. As Arendt argues, this kind of work could also result in the downfall of humanity's 'arts', "all human productivity would be sucked into an enormously intensified life process and would follow automatically, without pain or effort, its ever-recurrent natural cycle, i.e., its actual productivity".[242] Arendt primarily refers to the changes in work that were supposed to come with mechanization and automatization, but her thoughts from the 1950s also bear weight from the contemporary perspective. Arendt develops this thought on the basis of the classic differentiation between the spheres of human activity from Aristotle onwards. According to Virno, these spheres – work, creativity and political activity – are no longer fundamentally different. Virno states that the basic characteristic of contemporaneity and post-Fordist work is the disappearance of any differentiation between these three different types of activity. He focuses especially on the vanishing difference between work and politics: many traits of political activity constitute part of the post-Fordist world of work. In his interpretation, the public nature of work not only comprises the fact that everything has become work but also that work has taken over the traits of a public activity.

Contemporary and communicative work is a virtuoso kind of public work; it is performed for its own sake and it also generates a surplus value.[243] As mentioned several times in this book, the public and political nature of work profoundly mark the artistic work of today: artistic work should no longer be about creating, but about activity (or working with political, engaged and communicative human powers); the production of subjectivity, sociality and flexibility should be at its core. These powers become the powers of life and nature that are quite intense and extremely 'fertile' nowadays, accelerating the natural rhythm of life. According to Arendt, this does not change the basic character of this rhythm according to the world: "The rhythm of machines would magnify and intensify the natural rhythm of life enormously, but it would not change, only make more deadly, life's chief character with respect to the world, which is to wear down durability".[244]

The intense use of human powers destroys the tenacity, duration and persistence of the world, as well as the duration and persistence of subjectivity; for this reason, this use not only results in exhaustion and burn-out but also in the problematical subordination of our lives and activities to the ways of contemporary production. Art is therefore ambivalently close to capitalism. On the one hand, it is no longer exceptional; instead, it represents a way of seizing work to the fullest. On the other hand, it still indicates the material and embodied processes of creation that elude the necessity of life. Art is not useful and purposeful. It can result from a total coincidence or failure. The length of its duration is unforeseeable. Art lasts and is the potentiality of human powers that have not yet been realized. At the same time, art also does not belong to the intensification of the production of life. Quite the opposite, it is the anarchic force of waste, sleep and inactivity that opens up atmospheres and rhythms of life that are different from anything production-oriented. Because of its paradoxical autonomy, however, art is also fused with the entropy of life.

What might lie at the core of artistic autonomy is an awareness of the unrealized potentiality of creative powers; it opens up human activity and being to the kind of activity that is always less than it could be. The critical relationship between art and work could therefore be viewed through the prism of the possibility of working less; this does not concern lazy rebellion, the privilege of non-work or the extension of free time, but making it possible for artistic work to go on and on so that it can be, to paraphrase Agamben, work without qualities. It is this ability to do less, to endlessly persist in this 'less' and in what could be, that opens up the human being to the temporal dimension and makes it historical.

According to Heller Roazen, the human being owes its consistency to the possibility of being less than it is, which also gives human existence a temporal dimension: "To grasp a human action as such, one must look to the shadows of the more minor acts it inevitably projects around it: to those unaccomplished acts that are less than it and that could always have been performed in its stead, or, alternately, to those unaccomplished acts with respect to which it itself is less than it could have been."[245] It is the potentiality of doing less that gives tenacity to human activity and gives art the permanent and autonomous power to rethink the borders between the various types of human experience: art actually opens the gateway leading to this useless confirmation of life.

Doing less could also be understood as a new radical gesture that opens up speculation about the value of artistic life and, rather than working towards the perfection of work, starts working autonomously for life itself. It is therefore an important aesthetic and ethical attitude for the artist as a worker. This *less*, however, is uncompromising and performed on a grand scale: what can make human activities common to us all is the fact that we have the wonderful ability to do less and to do something other than what we could be doing.

Doing less also speaks of a specific attitude on the part of the artistic worker, who needs to withstand the creative speculations about his or her life in order to open up the temporal materiality of his or her own work. In this way, the artist's work yields to life, not in the sense of breaking the boundaries between life and artistic activity but always in the sense of placing its activity as the autonomous difference of a lesser act: it is enabling life through doing less. In this sense, doing less can be understood as an exceptionally important affective shift that can significantly influence the rhythmic and flexible atmospheres of contemporary artistic life and open up new ways of solidarity. This would then be the third disobedient line of argument in the defence of art: do less, precisely when confronted with the demand to do more.

Footnotes

1. Carey Young, "I'm the Revolutionary (2001)", *Incorporated*, London: Film and Video Umbrella, 2002, 173.
2. Slavoj Žižek, *Violence: Six Sideways Reflections*, London: Profile Books, 2009, 183.
3. The post-political state can be connected to the changes in post-industrial society. Many theorists state that the politics of today mainly involves the bureaucratic organization of everyday interests (Rancière), politics without antagonisms (Mouffe) or tightly connected to the changes in the mediatisation of politics as well as to economic and social changes (Baudrillard). We can also link the post-political state with the theories of Negri and Hardt, where the post-political is connected to the role of non-material work, the dominance of the empire and the changes in the perception of class ideologies.
4. Alain Badiou, "15 Theses on Art", *Maska*, 3-4, 19, (2005).
5. Olivier Marchart, "In Service of the Party. A Short Genealogy of Art and Collective Activism", *Maska*, 6-7, 21, (2006), pp. 88-99.
6. Ibidem, 94.
7. Ibidem, 99.
8. Chantal Mouffe, *On The Political*, London: Routledge, 2006, 72.
9. Ibidem, pp. 72-76.
10. Bojana Cvejić, *Learning by Making*, [online], Available from: http://summit.kein.org/node/235 (Accessed 26 January 2015).
11. Chantal Mouffe, *On The Political*, London: Routledge, 2006.
12. Jacques Rancière, *Disagreement. Politics and Philosophy*, Minneapolis: University of Minnesota Press, 1998, 28.
13. Jacques Rancière, *Aesthetics and its Discontents*, Hoboken:

John Wiley & Sons, 2009, 24.
14 Giorgio Agamben, *The Coming Community*, Minneapolis, London: University of Minnesota Press, 1993.
15 Jacques Rancière, *Aesthetics and its Discontents*, Hoboken: John Wiley & Sons, 2009, pp. 60-65.
16 Ibidem. 57.
17 Jacques Rancière, *Disagreement. Politics and Philosophy*, Minneapolis: University of Minnesota Press, 1998, 57.
18 Bojana Cvejić, *Learning by Making*, [online], Available from: http://summit.kein.org/node/235 (Accessed 26 January 2015).
19 Maurizio Lazzarato, "Conversation with Maurizio Lazzaratto: Exhausting Immaterial Labour in Performance", *Le Journal des Laboratoires and TKH*, 17, (October 2010), 14.
20 Bifo therefore states that we actually work with our souls today. Cf. Franco Berardi Bifo, *The Soul At Work. From Alienation to Autonomy*, New York: Semiotext(e), 2009, 21.
21 Cf. Antonin Artaud, *The Theater and Its Double*, New York: Grove Press, 1994. The notion of body without organs as an absence of the organisation of an organism is also one of the key notions in *Anti-Oedipus: Capitalism and Schizophrenia* by Deleuze and Guattari.
22 Suely Rolnik, *Life on the Spot*, [online], Available from: http://www.caosmose.net/suelyrolnik/index.html (Accessed 26 January 2015). Rolnik exhaustively describes the issues of this kind of transformation, basing her argument especially on the philosophy of subjectivity of Félix Guattari, who is also an important reference in Lazzarato's thought.
23 This is also discussed in the works of Robert Pfaller, *Das schmutzige Heilige und die reine Vernunft. Symptome der Gegenwartskultur*, Frankfurt am Main: Fischer Verlag, 2008. In his recent book, he compares such consumption with Freud's reflection on pleasure. Pleasure always exists, but

not always in a form full of pleasure. It can also exist as unconscious pleasure, which produces its own symptoms. In this way, we can actually enjoy without noticing it. Cf. *Wofür es sich zu leben lohnt. Elemente materialistischer Philosophie*, Frankfurt am Main: Fischer Verlag, 2011, 202.

24   This is the way that Derrida describes Artaud's desire in his essay 'The Theater of Cruelty and the Closure of Representation', in: *Theater Summer*, 9, 3, (1978), pp. 6-16.

25   Cf. Amelia Jones, *Body Art / Performing the Subject*, Minneapolis: University of Minnesota Press, 1998.

26   This is discussed by Erika Fischer Lichte, *The Transformative Power of Performance: A New Aesthetics*, New York: Routledge, 2008.

27   Brian Massumi, "Navigating Movements", *Hope*, M. Zaournazzi (Ed.), New York: Routledge, 2003, 224.

28   In the first seven years of their research work, Via Negativa focusses upon the thematisation of capital vices, or, in the researchers' words, seven 'negative' human traits: "Our outgoing point is that wrath, gluttony, greed, lust, sloth, envy and pride profoundly mark the identity of every individual. Each of these human characteristics opens up a conflict embedded in the subjectivity of every individual. On the one hand, it forms the mechanisms and strategies of defence against its negative drives. On the other hand, it develops various forms of lenience because it does not withstand the pressure of its own subjectivity." The second part of the research is called Via Nova; its last part deals with the theme of Shame. Cf. the studies in: *Ne, Via Negativa 2002–2008*, Marin Blažević (Ed.), Ljubljana: Maska, 2010.

29   In the High Fidelity scene of the performance *Incasso* (2004), the actor Grega Zorc first admits that, after the tragic accident of his parents, he was extremely happy to get some hifi music equipment, which he was able to purchase from the insurance money received after their deaths. After that,

he holds the heavy speakers, which were part of this equipment, in his extended arms until he can bear it no more. He physically needs to defeat the gravity of his own merchandise and greed. In the performance *Viva Mandič*, the actor Marko Mandič lists all of his major acting achievements and then literally squeezes out his acting potential and toasts himself with his own sweat after sweating for half an hour in a hermetically sealed bag, where, in the increasing heat and lack of air, his body produces so much sweat that he can drink it as a toast.

30 The public character of work is discussed in the last chapter, The Visibility of Work.
31 Michel Foucault, *The History of Sexuality*, New York: Random House LLC, 2012, 59.
32 Peter Klepec, *Dobičkonosne strasti: Kapitalizem in perverzija*, Ljubljana: Analecta, 2008.
33 Richard Sennett, *The Culture of the New Capitalism*, New Haven & London: Yale University Press, 2006, 123.
34 Max Weber, *The Protestant Ethic and the Spirit of Capitalism*, London: Routledge, 2001.
35 Paolo Virno, *A Grammar of the Multitude, For an Analysis of Contemporary Forms of Life*, New York: Semiote(x)te, 2004.
36 Agamben bases this argument on Foucault, whose works thoroughly analyse the dispositif as a creation of obeying yet free bodies, as the manner in which subjects accept their identities in the very process of subordination. In the English translation of his text dispositif is translated as apparatus.
37 Giorgio Agamben, *What is an apparatus? and Other Essays*, Stanford: Stanford University Press, 2009, 14.
38 Ibidem, 20.
39 Ibidem, 21.
40 This is discussed by Judith Butler, *Gender Trouble: Feminism and the Subversion of Identity*, New York – London:

Routledge, 2006.
41 Agamben, p. 8.
42 Ibidem, p. 18.
43 Ibidem, p. 30.
44 Giorgio Agamben, *Profanantions*, New York: Zone Books, 2010, 84.
45 Peter Klepec, *Dobičkonosne strasti: Kapitalizem in perverzija*. Ljubljana: Analecta, 2008.
46 Gullermo Gomez-Peña, *In defence of Performance Art*, [online], Available from: http://www.pochanostra.com/antes/jazz_pocha2/mainpages/in_defense.htm (Accessed 26 January 2015).
47 Agamben considers museums to cover not only artistic institutions, but also protected natural areas, tourist sights, etc. Cf. *Profanations*, New York: Zone Books, 2010.
48 Yvonne Rainer, *Letter to Marina Abramovic*, [online] Available from: http://theperformanceclub.org/2011/11/yvonne-rainer-douglas-crimpand-taisha-paggett-blast-marina-abramovic-and-moca-la/ (Accessed 26 January 2015).
49 Sarah Wookey, *An Open Letter from a Dancer who refused to participate in Marina Abramović's MOCA performance*, [online], Available from: http://www.blouinartinfo.com/news/story/751666/an-open-letter-from-a-dancer-who-refused-toparticipate-in-marina-abramovic%E2%80%99s-moca-performance (Accessed 26 January 2015).
50 The conversation between Marina Abramović and the art historian Sanford Kwinter is available from: http://youtu.be/iIL7stvnvBs (Accessed 26 January 2015).
51 Yvonne Rainer, *Letter to Marina Ambramović*, [online], Available from: http://theperformanceclub.org/2011/11/yvonne-rainer-douglascrimp-and-taisha-paggett-blast-marina-abramovic-and-moca-la/ (Accessed 26 January 2015).
52 This is the direction in which the performative shift and the

expansion of the performance art field into all social spheres should be rethought. This expansion is also discussed in by Jon McKenzie, *Perform or Else. From Discipline to Performance*, London: Routledge, 2001.

53 Sarah Wookey, *An Open Letter from a Dancer who refused to participate in Marina Abramović's MOCA performance*, [online], Available from: http://www.blouinartinfo.com/news/story/751666/an-open-letter-from-a-dancer-who-refused-toparticipate-in-marina-abramovic%E2%80%99s-moca-performance (Accessed 26 January 2015).

54 It is therefore not unusual that neoliberal governments display a strong desire to rename art 'creativity'; in this manner, human powers are exploited without a voice (without political antagonisms).

55 The problematic dimension of such reconstructions, especially feminist performance art pieces, is discussed by Martha Rosler: "If re-enactment brings us mystification rather than mytho-poesis, the performing of the Eternal Return, we have achieved the opposite of creative human freedom. When we see certain previously uncommodifed forms as switching from resistance to celebration, we can indeed fear that the second time is farce." Rosler's article points out the problematic status of the live archives and documentation of performance art pieces at museums; live archives can also be connected with the changes in contemporary subjectivity. Martha Rosler, *The Second Time as Farce*, [online], Idiom Magazine, Available from: http://idiommag.com/2011/02/the-second-time-as-farce/ (Accessed 26 January 2015).

56 Cf. for example: Boris Groys, *Gesamtkunstwerk Stalin. Die gespaltene Kultur in der Sowjiet Union*, Munich: Hanser, 1988. Cf. also the lecture [online]: *Repetition of Revolution, Russian Avantgarde Revisited*, Available from: http://www.formerwest.org/ResearchSeminars/RussianAvantgardeRevisited/V

ideo/RepetitionOfRevolution (Accessed 26 January 2015).
57 Slavoj Žižek, *Violence: Six Sideways Reflections*, London: Profile Books, 2009, 19.
58 Ibidem, 20.
59 Ibidem, 20
60 Jacques Lacan, *Television: A Challenge to the Psychoanalytic Establishment*, Edited by J. Copjec and translated by J. Mehlman, New York: W. W. Norton, 1990, 128.
61 Ibidem, 117.
62 Žižek discusses this in his book *Violence*, London: Profile Books, 2009.
63 Jacques-Alain Miller, "On Shame", *Jacques Lacan and the Other side of psychoanalysis*, Justin Clemens, Russell Grigg (Eds.), Durham: Duke University Press, 2006.
64 Eve Kosofsky Sedgwick, *Touching Feeling: Affect, Pedagogy, Performativity*, Durham, New York: Duke University Press, 2003, 38.
65 Alenka Zupančič, "Lacan in sram", *Problemi, Revija za kulturo in družbena vprašanja*, 44, 7/8, (2006), 99.
66 The political changes I have in mind are those of the political shift in 2010, especially under the influence of the positions of Geert Wilders's Party for Freedom, which supported the then minority government and introduced radical rightist political standpoints regarding the financing of the culture, the attitude towards minorities, health policy etc. One of the consequences of this shift was also the cultural and political programme *More than Quality*, drawn up by Halbe Zijlstra, the then Dutch delegate for education, culture and science. Despite the strong opposition of the people in the arts and the entire artistic sector, this programme of the Dutch state made substantial cuts in the area of culture and stopped the operation of numerous important, even key artistic and educational institutions, leaving the development of the arts entirely up to the market in many cases.

67 This was Kurt Weill's term for his opera *Mahagonny*, where the word 'Songspiel' was used as a derivative from the German word 'Singspiel'. The word denotes an operetta-like drama with musical dialogues.

68 The texts for the script are based on the actual notes of the then activists and reveal the hope and conception of the future on the one hand and the difficulties of building the society of the future together on the other.

69 *Victory over the Sun* was a Futurist avant-garde opera that saw its premiere in 1913.

70 Chantal Mouffe, *On The Political*, London: Routledge, 2006, 72.

71 The division of the sensual is discussed by Jacques Rancière in his book: *Dissensus: On Politics and Aesthetics*, London, New York: Continuum, 2010.

72 Nicolas Bourriaud, *Relational Aesthetics*, Dijon: Les presses du réel, 2002.

73 Ibidem, 14.

74 Claire Bishop, "Antagonism and Relational Aesthetics", *October*, 110, Autumn 2004, pp. 51–79. Look also: Claire Bishop: Artificial Hels, Participatory Arts and Politics of Spectatorship, Verso, 2012.

75 The problematic privileging of the active spectator in the philosophical reflection of theatre spectatorship is also discussed byJacques Rancière, "The Emancipated Spectator", *Artforum*, (March 2007), pp. 272-280.

76 Claire Bishop, "Antagonism and Relational Aesthetics", *October*, 110, Autumn 2004, p. 15.

77 Ibidem, p. 15.

78 Nicolas Bourriaud, *Relational Aesthetics*, Dijon: Les presses du réel, 2002.

79 Henri Lefebvre, *The Production of Space*, New York: John Wiley & Sons, 1991.

80 Jacques Rancière, "The Emancipated Spectator", *Artforum*,

(March 2007), pp. 272-280.
81 Beti Žerovc, "O umetniškem dogodku na umetniškem dogodku", Peter Kisin and Beti Žerovc (Eds.), *29. grafični bienale Ljubljana: Dogodek / The 29th Biennial of Graphic Arts: The Event*, Ljubljana: Mednarodni grafični likovni center / International Centre of Graphic Arts, 2011, p. 13.
82 Hito Steyerl, "Is a Museum a Factory?", *e-flux Journal*, 7, June - August 2009, pp. 5-10. Also available from: http://www.e-flux.com/journal/is-a-museum-a-factory.
83 Ibidem. pp. 3-10.
84 Ibidem. pp. 3-10.
85 Nicolas Bourriaud, *Relational Aesthetics*, Dijon: Les presses du réel, 2002.
86 Irit Rogoff, *We - Collectivites, Mutualities, Participations*, [online], Available from: http://theater.kein.org/node/95 (Accessed 26 January 2015).
87 Sonja Lavaert, Pascal Gielen, "The Dismeasure of Art. An Interview with Paolo Virno", *Open 17: A Precarious Existence. Vulnerability in the Public Domain*, Amsterdam: SKOR (Foundation Art and Public Space), 17, (2009).
88 Hito Steyerl: "Is a Museum a Factory?", *e-flux Journal* 7, June–August 2009, pp. 5-10. Also available from: http://www.e-flux.com/journal/is-a-museum-a-factory.
89 Sonja Lavaert, Pascal Gielen, "The Dismeasure of Art. An Interview with Paolo Virno", *Open 17: A Precarious Existence. Vulnerability in the Public Domain*, Amsterdam: SKOR (Foundation Art and Public Space), 17, (2009). Also available from: http://www.skor.nl/article-4178-en.html (Accessed 26 January 2015).
90 Ibidem.
91 Jacques Rancière, "The Emancipated Spectator", *Artforum*, (March 2007), pp. 272-280.
92 Ibidem, 279.
93 Peter Gena, Jonathan Brent (Eds.), *A John Cage Reader: In*

Celebration of His Seventieth Birthday, New York: C. F. Peters, 1982, 22.
94 Renata Salecl, "Zadnje predavanje (The Last Lecture)", *Delo*, March 3, 2008, 40.
95 Ibidem. Pausch bravely fought his illness, but succumbed to it in July 2008.
96 Fredric Jameson, *Postmodernism, Or the Cultural Logic of Late Capitalism*, Durham, New York: Duke University Press, 1999.
97 Andrew Carnegie, Quoted from: Florian Schneider, *Collaboration*, [online], Available from: http://summit.kein.org/node/190 (Accessed 26 January 2015).
98 Florian Schneider, *Collaboration*, [online], Available from: http://summit.kein.org/node/190 (Accessed 26 January 2015).
99 Matteo Pasquinelli, *Immaterial Civil War, Prototypes of Conflict within Cognitive Capitalism*, [online], Available from: http://eipcp.net/policies/cci/pasquinelli/en (Accessed 26 January 2015).
100 Florian Schneider, *Collaboration*, [online], Available from: http://summit.kein.org/node/190 (Accessed 26 January 2015).
101 Paolo Virno, *A Grammar of the Multitude: For an Analysis of Contemporary Forms of Life*, New York: Semiotext(e), 2004, 41.
102 Ibidem., 41.
103 Ibidem., 41.
104 Hito Steyerl, "Forget Otherness", *Another Publication*, Renee Ridgway, Katarina Zdjelar (Eds.), Berlin: Revolver, 2006, pp. 15-20.
105 Eleanor Bauer, "Becoming Room, Becoming Mac, New Artistic Identities in the Transnational Brussels Dance Community", *Maska*, 22, 107-108, (2007), 66.
106 Myriam Van Imschoot, Xavier Le Roy, "Letters in Collaboration", *Maska*, 1-2 (84-85), 2004, 54.

107 André Lepecki, "Dance without distance", *Ballet International / Tanz Aktuell*, February 2001, pp. 29-31.
108 Myriam Van Imschoot, Xavier Le Roy, "Letters in Collaboration", *Maska*, 1-2 (84-85), 2004, 54.
109 Charles Green, *The Third Hand, Collaboration in Art from Modernism to Postmodernism*, Kensington: University of New South Wales Press, 2001.
110 Florian Schneider, *Collaboration*, [online], Available from: http://summit.kein.org/node/190 (Accessed 26 January 2015).
111 Cf. http://www.everybodystoolbox.net.
112 This is also discussed by Jodi Dean, who lucidly analyses the capitalisation of the communication and collaboration in new media. Cf. Jodi Dean, *Blog Theory, Feedback and Capture in the Circuits of Drive*, London: Polity Press, 2010.
113 Myriam Van Imschoot, Xavier Le Roy, "Letters in Collaboration", *Maska*, 1-2 (84-85), 2004, 55.
114 Alain Badiou, "15 Theses on Art", *Maska*, 3-4, 19, (2005), 9.
115 Slavoj Žižek, Violence: Six Sideways Reflections, London: Profile Books, 2009.
116 Marx's letter to Arnold Ruge, 1844.
117 Leland de la Durantaye, "Agamben's Potential", *Diacritics*, 30, 2 (Summer 2000), pp. 3-24.
118 Giorgio Agamben, *The Coming Community*, Minneapolis: University of Minnesota Press, 1993.
119 This is also how this text on working together was created. In 2007, I was supposed to give a lecture together with Ivana Müller on the prognosis of working together at a conference in Berlin, but our co-operation failed to materialise. Although we wanted that very much, we ran out of time. When writing the text, I realised that we failed because we wished to invent and make visible yet another protocol of cooperation and add yet more to its excess. We did not consider that we were already cooperating, meeting, posing

each other challenges through numerous situations and conditioning our common future, in which visibility hardly plays a part at all.
120 Simon Ford, *The Situationists International*, London: Black Dog Publishing, 2005, 42.
121 Susan Buck-Morrs, *Dreamworld and Catastrophe. The Passing of Mass Utopia in East and West*, Cambridge, Massachusetts, London: The MIT Press, 2002.
122 Allan Kaprow, "Notes on the creation of a Total Art", *Critical Mass: Happenings, Fluxus, Performance, Intermedia and Rutgers University*, New Brunswick: Rutgers University Press, 2003, 6.
123 Jean-Luc Nancy, *The Inoperative Community*, Peter Connor (Ed.), Minneapolis, London: University of Minessota Press, 2004, XIII.
124 Ibidem, XXXIX.
125 The exhibition: *Collective Creativity*, curating: What, How & for Whom / WHW (Ana Devic, Nataša Ilic, Sabina Sabolovic, Ivet Curlin), Kunsthalle Fridericianum, Kassel, May 1 – July 17, 2005. Chto Delat? / What is to be done?, a group of artists and theorists of the younger generation, consisting of artists (Tsaplya and Glucklya, Nikolai Oleinikov, Kirill Shuvalov and Dmitry Vilensky), philosophers (Artem Magun, Oxana Timofeeva, Alexei Penzin) and writers (David Riff, Alexander Skidan) active in St. Petersburg, Moscow, Nizhny Novgorod and Berlin. The group was founded in 2003 with the action *The Refoundation of Petersburg*. http://chtodelat.org
126 The text from *The Builders* video is available at: http://vimeo.com/6878627.
127 Over the last few years, there have been many exhibitions on the theme of community as well as perofrmances dealing with the subject of collaboration. An example would be *Colect-if* (2003) by a group of seven artistic creators (Bojana

Cvejić, Varinia Canto Villa, Alix Eynaudi, Ugo Dahaes, Katarina Stegnar, Rebecca Murgi and Janez Janša).
128 Jean-Luc Nancy, *The Inoperative Community*, Peter Connor (Ed.), Minneapolis, London: University of Minnesota Press, 2004, XIII.
129 Ibidem.
130 Jean-Luc Nancy, *The Inoperative Community*, Peter Connor (Ed.), Minneapolis, London: University of Minnesota Press, 2004, XXXIX.
131 Jean-Baptiste Marongiu, "Agamben, le chercheur d'homme", *Libération*, April 1, 1999. The interview is also available at: http://www.liberation.fr/livres/1999/04/01/agamben-le-chercheur-d-homme_270036 (Accessed 26 January 2015)
132 Giorgio Agamben, *The Coming Community*, Minneapolis, London: University of Minnesota Press, 1993.
133 Leland de la Durantaye, "Agamben's Potential", *Diacritics*,30, 2 (Summer 2000), pp. 3-24.
134 BADco. is a collaborative performance collective based in Zagreb, Croatia. The artistic core of the collective are Pravdan Devlahovic, Ivana Ivković, Ana Kreitmeyer, Tomislav Medak, Goran Sergej Pristaš, Nikolina Pristaš and Zrinka Užbinec.
135 Harun Farocki, Arbeiter Verlassen die Fabrik, video, 36 min, 1995.
136 Harun Farocki, "Workers Leaving the Factory", BADco. *1 poor and one 0*, Zagreb: theatre programme of the performance, 2008.
137 Bojana Cvejić, *How open are you open? Pre-sentiments, pre-conceptions, pro-jections*, [online], 2004, Available from: http://www.sarma.be/text.asp?id=1113 (Accessed 26 January 2015).
138 Ibidem.
139 Cf. also Randy Martin, *Critical Moves. Dance Studies in Theory*

and Politics, Durham, New York: Duke University Press, 1998. For a more historical approach to the connection between dance and work from the American perspective, cf. Mark Franko, *The Work of Dance. Labour, Movement and Identity in the 1930s*, Middletown: Wesleyan Press, 2002.

140 John Martin, *The Modern Dance*, Hightstown: Dance Horizons, 1990.

141 A. K. Gastev, "The Song of the Workers' Blow", in: Aleksandr Bogdanov, "Proletarian Poetry", *The Labour Monthly*, (June 1932), 357.

142 Gerald Raunig, *A Thousand Machines*, New York: Semiotext(e), 2010.

143 The aspects of the kinetic ideologies of modernity are analysed in André Lepecki, *Exhausting Dance, Performance and the Politics of Movement*, New York: Routledge Champan and Hall, 2006.

144 This has several consequences, which we will not deal with in great detail. Firstly, the pleasure of working bodies is reproduced in a new form of capitalist work – entertainment and spectacle, e.g. in the dancing bodies of the Tiller Girls or the dance compositions of Busby Berkeley. Secondly, dance resurfaces in the massive spectacles of 'natural bodies', in which movement is interiorized as the (only) nature of the human body, making the healthy and powerful moving person part of the naturalised masses of totalitarian systems.

145 Dr. Seuss: *Pontoffel Pock, Where Are You*, DVD, Universal Studios, 2003 (25 min).

146 Natalie Bookchin, *Mass Ornament*, 2006. The video is available at: http://vimeo.com/5403546 (Accessed 26 January 2015). Of course, Bookchin refers to the eminent essay *The Mass Ornament* by Siegfried Kracauer.

147 Brian Massumi, *The Future Birth of the Affective Fact*, [online], Conference Proceedings: Genealogies of Biopolitics,

Available from: http://browse.reticular.info/text/collected/massumi.pdf (Accessed 26 January 2015).
148 This centrality of movement in Post-Fordistic production has also been overlooked when the cognitive proletariat was understood by philosophers to be a new force in the political battle against the forces of capital, as a possibility for a new political movement. The problem is that such a cognitive proletariat is actually highly disembodied, already colonised through the temporality of accelerated and quantitative movement, or as Franco Birardi Bifo writes: cognitarians still have to search for the body. Franco Berardi Bifo, *Cognitarian Subjectivation*, [online], e-flux Journal (2010), Available from: http://www.e-flux.com/journal/cognitariansubjectivation (Accessed 26 January 2015).
149 Paolo Virno, *The Dismeasure of Art*, [online], Open, A Precarious Existence, 17 (2009), Availabe from: http://www.skor.nl/article-4178-en.html (Accessed 26 January 2015).
150 From the history of the Skype chat of Igor Štromajer and Brane Zorman at the time of transmission of *Ballettikka Internettikka: Stattikka*. The documentation of the project is available from: http://www.intima.org/bi/stattikka (Accessed 26 January 2015).
151 *Tele-Plateaus – Performative Installation* was a special event created by Johannes Birringer, Klaus Nicolai and Thomas Dumke and was presented as a part of the CYNET Festival in Hellerau Hall, Dresden (2007).
152 Agamben describes observers of chronological time in: Giorgio Agamben, *The Time That Remains, A Commentary on the Letter to the Romans*, Redwood: Stanford University Press, 2005.
153 I will deal with this in more detail in the last chapter.
154 Cristina Demaria, *nvsbl*, [online], Available from: http://www.eszter-salamon.com/WWW/nvsbl.htm (Accessed 26 January 2015).

155 Maurice Blanchot, *The Infinite Conversation*, Minneapolis: University of Minnesota Press, 1992, 121.
156 Cf. Hans-Ties Lehmann, *Postdramatic Theatre*, London: Routledge, 2006.
157 Adrian Heathfield, *Out of Now, The Lifeworks of Tehching Hsieh*, Cambridge, Massachusetts: The MIT Press, 2009.
158 I will discuss this in more detail in the chapter The Artist's Time: Projective Temporality.
159 Just as the body needs to forget about its home bed in order to be able to sleep in it peacefully.
160 Maurice Blanchot, *The Infinite Conversation*, Minneapolis: University of Minnesota Press, 1992, 121.
161 The awareness of the potential temporality of work is at the core of many time procedures in art. According to art historian Pamela M. Lee, they constitute a response to the new feeling of the end of history and the endless acceleration of the future, which marks an important part of the art of the 1960s. As Lee states, it is the questions on time that are the heir to the artistic explorations of the 1960s. In that period, art not only faces changed historical concepts of time, but also changed time rythms and modulations under the influence of technological development. Lee uses the concepts of durarion and infinity to analyse films by Andy Warhol (*Kiss, Sleep, Empire*) and the meticulously timed processes of durational painting by the artist On Kawara. Pamela M. Lee, *Chronophobia, On Time in the Art of the 1960s*, Cambridge, London: The MIT Press, 2006.
162 Cf. Peter Sloterdijk, "Eurotaoism, to a critique of political kinetics", *Nietzsche and the Rhetoric of Nihilism: Essays on Interpretation, Language and Politics*, Tom Darby, Béla Egyed, Ben Jones (Eds.), Ottawa: Carleton University Press, 1989, 99-116.
163 Gilles Deleuze, *Bergsonism*, New York: Zone Books, 1991, 48.
164 Ibidem, 48.

165 Odo Marquard, *Temporales Doppelleben: Philosophische Bemerkugen zu unserer Zeit*, Jahburch 1990 der Deutschen Akademie für Sprache und Dichtung, Wiesbaden: Luchterland, 1990.

166 Dieter Lesage, "Portrait of the Artist as a Worker", *Maska*, 5-6, 20, (2006), pp. 91-92. Cf. also a more detailed publication: Dieter Lesage, *Portrait of the Artist as a DJ, Notes on Ina Wudtke*, Brussels: VHD, 2008. Lesage later continued this analysis in a series of other essays: "Portrait of an artist as a resident", *Etcetera*, 24, 104, pp. 22-23, Brussels: Theaterpublicaties, (2006) and "Portrait of an artist as a researcher", *A Visual Culture Quarterly*, 179, 29, pp. 1-152, Antwerp: MuHKA, (2007).

167 Paolo Virno, *A Grammar of the Multitude: For an Analysis of Contemporary Forms of Life*, New York: Semiotext(e), 2004.

168 Nicolas Bourriaud, *Relational Aesthetics*, Dijon: Les presses du réel, 2002. Lesage is highly critical of the simplified formal approach to the practice of DJ-ing as found in Bourriaud, who fails to consider its social and political moments. A similarly rhetorical redirection of the notion can be found in another of Bourriaud's essays, created as a response to Rancière's criticism of his views. Bourriaud views the pracarity of artistic works as a new formal openness of art, in which he entirely abstracts their economical and social dimensions. Cf. Nicolas Bourriaud, *Precarious Constructions. Answer on Jacques Rancière on Art and Politics*, [online], Available from: http://classic.skor.nl/articicle-4416-nl.html?lang=en (Accessed 26 January 2015).

169 Paolo Virno, *A Grammar of the Multitude: For an Analysis of Contemporary Forms of Life*, New York: Semiotext(e), 2004, 63.

170 Luc Boltanski, Eve Chiapello, *The New Spirit of Capitalism*, London: Verso, 2007.

171 As warned by Ivor Southwood, this requirement not only holds for those who have work, but also for those who don't;

the unemployed must constantly prove their employability, be in a state of constant readiness, educate themselves and organize their empty time as if they actually had full-time employment. In this, subjectivity is wholly fused with work; the absence of work is nothing but constantly claiming that we are working on getting work – the performance of the working visibility of the absence of work. Ivor Southwood, *Non Stop Inertia*, London: Zero Books, 2011.

172 This kind of virtuosic speculation characterizes the entire projective creative work and frames artistic work into a very special kind of temporality. I discuss this in more detail in the subchapter "The Artist's Time: Projective Temporality".

173 Lauren Berlant, *Cruel Optimism*, Durham, New York: Duke University Press, 2011.

174 Ibidem.

175 This is discussed in more detail in Chapter Two: "The Production of Sociality".

176 Vassilis Tsianos, Dimitris Papadopoulos, *Precarity: A Savage Journey to the Heart of Embodied Capitalism*, [online], Available from: http://eipcp.net/transversal/1106/tsianospapadopoulos/en (Accessed 26 January 2015).

177 This world is not only outside the 'rich' world; parallel to the visible work of Google's creative labs, whose architectural concept and 'free' creative work represent some sort of ideal disappearance of the difference between work time and free time, there exists the 'invisible' Fordist work of the data inputers and cheap IT work force working under strict security conditions and entitled to a lot less benefits than Google's creative staff.

178 Walter Benjamin, *The Author as Producer*, [online], New Left Review, I/62, (1970), and Available from: http://ebookbrowsee.net/walter-benjamin-the-author-as-producer-pdf-d223630935 (Accessed 26 January 2015).

179 Ibidem.

180 Ibidem.
181 What else should this added value of artistic life be but the ideal image that it is possible to live in a free and relaxed manner while working a lot, so that the difference between work and life no longer matters? This added value also furthers the gentrification processes in contemporary cities. Artists, whose lifestyle represents an ideal to those who 'work', in terms that it is possible to lead a working life and work as an artist, often inhabit the poorest urban areas, which later become resident centres for the upper middle class.
182 Marion Von Osten, "Irene ist Viele! Or What We Call 'Productive Forces'", *e-flux Journal*, (September 2009), 8.
183 Ibidem, 9.
184 Ibidem, 7.
185 Marion Von Osten, "Irene ist Viele! Or What We Call 'Productive Forces'", *e-flux Journal*, (September 2009), 8.
186 The more central creativity is in production, the more it is reduced, disciplined and regulated. Today, this is especially evident in the numerous higher education reforms: a so-called knowledge-based society develops countless mechanisms by means of which creativity is regulated and made to fit transparent 'moulds', whose effectiveness must be open to verification at any given moment.
187 This kind of 'unworthiness of life' often underlies the argumentation of political reforms, especially in a time of economic crisis: suddenly, a number of professions and types of work are no longer profitable; for this reason, they are no longer worthy of 'life'. They are subjugated to austerity principles as if life can be tightened like a belt and frozen for a while.
188 Jacques Rancière, *The Politics of Aesthetics, The Distribution of the Sensible*, London, New York: Continuum, 2004, 23.
189 Ibidem, 45.

190 Ibidem, 45.
191 Luc Boltanski, Eve Chiapello, *The New Spirit of Capitalism*, London: Verso, 2007.
192 Lauren Berlant, *Cruel Optimism*, Durham, New York: Duke University Press, 2011.
193 Stefano Harney, Valentina Desideri, *Fate Work: A Conversation*, [online], Ephemera, Theory & Politics of Organization, Available from: http://www.ephemera-journal.org/contribution/fate-work-conversation (Accessed 26 January 2015).
194 As Le Roy explains in his performance, it was actually about Charmatz's reaction to Le Roy's promise; the invitation was therefore meant as a challenge to Le Roy.
195 The stringing of projects is connected with the acceleration of time, well-illustrated by the German sociologist Harmut Rosa using two metaphors. If the cultural image of the liberating and accelerated speed of the 20th century was that of a motorcycle then, in Rosa's opinion, the freedom of the motorcyclist has now been replaced by a hamster endlessly turning its treadmill wheel in a static place. And we know what happens to the motorcycle wheel if it keeps spinning and the machine is held in place. Cf. *Full Speed Burnout? From the Pleasures of the Motorcycle to the Bleakness of the Treadmill: The Dual Face of Social Acceleration*, [online], International Journal of Motorcycle Studies, 6, 1, (Summer 2010), Available from: http://ijms.nova.edu/Spring2010/IJMS_Artcl.Rosa.html (Accessed 26 January 2015).
196 The spectator's pleasure in turning one's own working conditions upside down can be compared to the strategies and tactics of laziness, which does not stand for non-work, but notably for a different form of consumption. This is humorously and cynically discussed by the French psychoanalyst Corinne Maier in *Bonjour Laziness* (*Bonjour Paresse*, 2004), which describes various ways of not doing any work

within corporate culture. Cf. Corinne Maier, *Bonjour Paresse*, Paris: Michalon, 2004. The theme of this book compels me to quote one of the rules stated: "Be kind to people on temporary contracts. They are the only ones who actually work."

197 Simon Bayly, "The End of the Project: Futurity in the Culture of Catastrophe", *Angelaki: Journal of the Theoretical Humanities*, 2, 18, (2013).

198 This unfinished nature is present in the project in a very interesting way. Bayly gives the example of a contemporary scientist working in the field of nanotechnology, robotics or artificial intelligence. The essential part of his work is that the project should not end in accordance with the predictions in the project proposal: the success of the project is measured in terms of whether the results actually exceed the expectations; artificial intelligence must therefore do precisely what we do not expect it to.

199 Johnnie Gratton, Michael Sheringam (Eds.), *The Art of the Project*, Oxford: Berg Hahn Books, 2005.

200 This is why the politics of time can be one of essential resistance dimensions of art; its resistance to the growing number of projects shows a completely different understanding of production and consumption. One of these works is definitely *Noordung* by the director Dragan Živadinov, characterized by a different project logic with a sustainable attitude towards time. *Noordung* does not take place as the transformation of one work into another, but as a holistic concept of the future, which cannot be implemented in any other way than by means of a radical revaluation of the duration of artistic work. Paradoxically, this duration restores artistic work to the present, leaving material traces on the work itself. There is another thing in this project that separates it from projective temporality: this project is not marked by catastrophe but predominantly by

a utopian affirmation of the future, in which the deadline is not only a work amendment, but a vision of life.

201 The word 'project' comes from the Latin word 'proiectum', which means 'before an action'.

202 This is discussed by Marx in *Capital* in connection with the 'species-essence' (Gattungswesen) of the human being; work is connected with the collective condition of existence.

203 Jason Read, "The Production of Subjectivity: From Transindividuality to the Commons", *New Formations: A Journal of Culture/Theory/Politics*, 70, (2010).

204 André Gorz, *Critique of Economic Reason*, London: Verso, 1990.

205 Boyan Manchev, "Performance time or time of performance? The struggle for duration as struggle for the event", *Maska: Projective Temporality*, 149-150, XXVII (2012), pp. 118-121.

206 The rebellion of the art of the 1960s against the capitalisation of human abilities is also discussed by Pamela M. Lee in her research on the temporality of 1960s art. The author focusses on the obsession with time in the art of the 1960s in order to shed light on various temporal politics of art and stresses the need to a different understanding of the present. Cf. Pamela M. Lee, *Chronophobia, On Time in the Art of the 1960s*, Cambridge, London: MIT Press, 2006.

207 The problems of this difference are also discussed by Maurizio Lazzarato himself, who actually launched the notion of immaterial work in the 1990s. Cf. Maurizio Lazzarato, "Conversation with Maurizio Lazzaratto, Exhausting Immaterial Labour in Performance", *Le Journal des Laboratoires and TKH*, 17, (October 2010).

208 Simon Bayly, "The End of the Project: Futurity in the Culture of Catastrophe", *Angelaki: Journal of the Theoretical Humanities*, 18, 2, (2013).

209 Maurizio Lazzarato, *The Making of the Indebted Man*, New

York: Semiotext(e), 2012.
210 This new feeling also gives rise to new symptoms: burn-out, chronic fatigue syndrome and depression. For this reason, e.g. Mark Fischer places mental problems and illnesses connected with the feeling of the appropriation of any kind of authenticity, the inability to do something new and constant flexibility, at the very centre of the new style of late capitalism, which he terms capitalist realism. According to Fischer, capitalist realism demands that we yield to reality, which is plastic and capable of reconfiguration at any given moment. Cf. Mark Fisher, *Capitalist Realism*, London: Zero Books, Verso, 2009.
211 Henri Lefebvre, *The Critique of Everyday Life, Foundations for the Sociology of Everyday*, New York – London: Verso, 2002, 183.
212 Boris Groys, "The Loneliness of the Project", *Going Public*, Berlin: Sternberg Press, 2010, 75.
213 Ibidem, 72.
214 The solipsism in choreographic practices and the role of the idiot is discussed by André Lepecki in his analysis by ASGAMA, a performance by Juan Dominguez and early performances by Bruce Nauman. Cf. André Lepecki, *Exhausting Dance, Performance and the Politics of Movement*, New York: Routledge, Champan and Hall, 2006.
215 For this reason, a lot of 1960s and 1970s performance art pieces were like tests – of endurance, recognition, code cracking etc. Early happenings were based on meticulous scripts of actions. It was these meticulous protocols that opened art to the project.
216 Boris Groys, "The Loneliness of the Project", *Going Public*, Berlin: Sternberg Press, 2010, 75.
217 Jason Read: "The Production of Subjectivity: From Transindividuality to the Commons", *New Formations: A Journal of Culture/Theory/Politics*, 70, (July 7, 2010), 125. We

could say that we actually spend our social powers as loners. This is also why it is possible to work with contemporary means of communication in utter loneliness; today, this kind of isolation is actually the most sociable.

218 Chris Burden, *Documentation of Selected Works 1971–1975*, film, 35 min. Available from: http://www.ubu.com/film/burden.html (Accessed 26 January 2015).

219 Boris Groys, "The Loneliness of the Project", *Going Public*, Berlin: Sternberg Press, 2010, 78.

220 Ibidem, 79. Let me add that, paradoxically, this documentation also points to the fascination and phantasms of contemporary bio-power. In his latest novel, *The Map and the Territory* (2010), Michel Houellebecq describes Jed Martin, an artist whose artistic projects offer different perspectives on work. In his young years, Martin focusses on industrial work and, as an established artist, he primarily studies the division of labour in contemporary capitalism. In the novel, Jed approaches Houellebecq himself so that the latter can write a review on yet another in Jed's series of extremely economically successful works. Houellebecq describes Martin as an ethnographer rather than a political commentator. This ethnographical role of the artist (also dealt with by Hal Foster in his famous essay *The Artist as an Ethnographer*) points out the bio-political status of contemporary art and its documentation of life. The fact that art wants to be life gives art a speculative value.

221 Simon Bayly, "The End of the Project: Futurity in the Culture of Catastrophe", *Angelaki: Journal of the Theoretical Humanities*, 18, 2, (2013).

222 This is discussed in: Renata Salecl, *The Tyranny of Choice*, London: Profile Books, 2011.

223 The problem is all the more acute because in many countries, the common only exists at the symbolic, national level, and whenever the arts are under fire, the argument in

their defence is the problematic and homely notion of 'culture'. It is argued that the arts are the good, humane, civilized kernel under the surface of brutal capitalist inhumanity, which only gives rise to a moral discussion, in terms of the good and the bad, with the argument taking the wrong direction.

224 There needs to be a differentiation between economically successful artists who can generate an enormous fictitious value (like by example Damien Hirst) and the remaining artistic production, which operates under completely different economic conditions. The dependence of the arts on financial speculation is not really part of my discussion since I am more interested in the wider and financially less successful artistic production (still subject to market principles), which is far from the speculative excesses of the art market. Nevertheless, such speculations do testify to a basic irrationality of value and confirm that art has very little to do with economic value; its value chiefly results from irrational expectations. This is also the reason for the great number of intermediators, whose task is to constantly establish, check and contextualize the value of art.

225 Robert Pfaller, *Wofür es sich zu leben lohnt, Elemente materialistischer Philosophie,* Frankfurt am Main: Fischer Verlag, 2011.

226 Ibidem, 202.

227 Ibidem, 203.

228 Ibidem, 204.

229 The notion of rationalization can be placed parallel to the notion of transparency; they both reflect the desire of the contemporary capitalist economy to prove itself to be as rational as possible, with any use and consumption being goal-oriented. This obsessive need for rationalization springs from the irrational nature of this economy – that of increasing and constant production, where excessive profit arises from the consumption of the surplus. There is no

pleasure left in this kind of consumption. Furthermore, rationality in the contemporary economy goes hand in hand with a bad conscience; we always buy too much of what is supposedly good for us and nature.
230 Pfaller, 205.
231 Ibidem, 205.
232 Ibidem, 205.
233 Mladen Stilinović, *Artist at work: 1973–1983 = Umetnik na delu: 1973–1983*, Ljubljana: ŠKUC Gallery, 2005.
234 Ibidem.
235 Of course, this not only holds for visual art but also for contemporary dance and experimental theatre forms.
236 Cf. e.g. *East Art Map, Contemporary Art and Eastern Europe*, Irwin (Ed.), London: Afterall, 2006.
237 Aaron Schuster, *Zelo težko je početi nič*, [online], Dnevnikov Objektiv, Maša Ogrizek, (1 October 2011), Available from: http://www.dnevnik.si/objektiv/intervjuji/1042476800 (Accessed 26 January 2015).
238 Hannah Arendt, *The Human Condition*, Chicago, London: The University of Chicago Press, 1998, 128.
239 Ibidem, 173.
240 Ibidem, 127.
241 This is also how projective temporality operates: the life processes are made more intense by means of projects.
242 Arendt, 129.
243 Virno's statement on surplus value is key to understanding the changes in post-Fordist work and also poses the difference to Marx's understanding of virtuoso work. In post-Fordism, the work considered by Marx as personal services becomes work into which capital is invested: industry changes into a communication industry and the shaping of factories of ideas. I can also connect the surplus value of virtuoso work with my own statement on the speculative value of artistic life: what is invested in is not art

but artistic and creative powers: the artist's life is at the core of the interest on the capital.
244 Arendt, 134.
245 Daniel Heller Roazen, *Echolalias, On the Forgetting of Language*, New York: Zone Books, 2005. Heller Roazen develops this thought on the basis of reading the ninth-century scholar al-JãAiA In his monumental work *Book of Animals,* al-JãAiA reflects on the difference between animal and man.

Bibliography

Giorgio Agamben, *Profanantions*, New York: Zone Books, 2010.

Giorgio Agamben, *The Coming Community*, Minneapolis, London: University of Minnesota Press, 1993.

Giorgio Agamben, *The Time That Remains, A Commentary on the Letter to the Romans*, Redwood: Stanford University Press, 2005.

Giorgio Agamben, *What is an apparatus? and Other Essays*, Stanford: Stanford University Press, 2009.

Hannah Arendt, *The Human Condition*, Chicago, London: The University of Chicago Press, 1998.

Antonin Artaud, *The Theater and Its Double*, New York: Grove Press, 1994.

Alain Badiou, "15 Theses on Art", *Maska*, 3-4, 19, (2005).

Eleanor Bauer, "Becoming Room, Becoming Mac, New Artistic Identities in the Transnational Brussels Dance Community", *Maska*, 22, 107-108, (2007).

Simon Bayly, "The End of the Project: Futurity in the Culture of Catastrophe", *Angelaki: Journal of the Theoretical Humanities*, 18, 2, (2013).

Walter Benjamin, "The Author as Producer", [online], *New Left Review*, I/62, (1970), Available from: http://ebookbrowsee.net/walter-benjamin-the-author-as-producer-pdf-d223630935 (Accessed 26 January 2015).

Franco Berardi Bifo, Cognitarian Subjectivation, [online], *e-flux Journal*, (2010), Available from: http://www.e-flux.com/journal/cognitarian-subjectivation (Accessed 26 January 2015).

Franco Berardi Bifo, *The Soul At Work. From Alienation to Autonomy*, New York: Semiotext(e), 2009.

Lauren Berlant, *Cruel Optimism*, Durham, New York: Duke University Press, 2011.

Claire Bishop, "Antagonism and Relational Aesthetics", *October*, 110, Autumn 2004. Also available from: http://www.marginalutility.org/wp-content/uploads/2010/07/Claire-Bishop_Antagonism-and-Relational-Aesthetics.pdf (Accessed 26 January 2015).

Maurice Blanchot, *The Infinite Conversation*, Minneapolis: University of Minnesota Press, 1992.

Marin Blažević (Ed.), *Ne, Via Negativa 2002–2008*, Ljubljana: Maska, 2010.

Luc Boltanski, Eve Chiapello, *The New Spirit of Capitalism*, London: Verso, 2007.

Nicolas Bourriaud, "Precarious Constructions. Answer on Jacques Rancière on Art and Politics", [online], Availablre from: http://classic.skor.nl/article-4416-nl.html?lang=en (Accessed 26 January 2015).

Nicolas Bourriaud, *Relational Aesthetics*, Dijon: Les presses du réel, 2002.

Susan Buck-Morrs, *Dreamworld and Catastrophe. The Passing of Mass Utopia in East and West*, Cambridge, Massachusetts, London: The MIT Press, 2002.

Judith Butler, *Gender Trouble: Feminism and the Subversion of Identity*, New York, London: Routledge, 2006.

Bojana Cvejić, "How open are you open? Pre-sentiments, pre-conceptions, pro-jections", [online], 2004, Available from: http://www.sarma.be/text.asp?id=1113 (Accessed 26 January 2015).

Bojana Cvejić, "Learning by Making", [online], Available from: http://summit.kein.org/node/235 (Accessed 26 January 2015).

Jodi Dean, *Blog Theory, Feedback and Capture in the Circuits of Drive*, London: Polity Press, 2010.

Gilles Deleuze, Felix Guattari, *Anti-Oedipus: Capitalism and Schizophrenia*, Minneapolis: University of Minnesota Press, 1983.

Gilles Deleuze, *Bergsonism*, New York: Zone Books, 1991.

Cristina Demaria, "nvsbl", [online], Available from: http://www.eszter-salamon.com/WWW/nvsbl.htm (Accessed 26 January 2015).

Jacques Derrida, "The Theater of Cruelty and the Closure of Representation", *Theater Summer*, 9, 3, (1978).

Leland de la Durantaye, "Agamben's Potential", *Diacritics*, 30, 2 (Summer 2000).

Harun Farocki, "Workers Leaving the Factory", BADco. *1 poor and one 0*, Zagreb: theatre programme of the performance, 2008.

Mark Fisher, *Capitalist Realism*, London: Zero Books, Verso, 2009.

Erika Fischer Lichte, The Transformative Power of Performance: A New Aesthetics, New York: Routlege, 2008.

Simon Ford, *The Situationists International*, London: Black Dog Publishing, 2005.

Michel Foucault, *The History of Sexuality*, New York: Random House LLC, 2012.

Mark Franko, *The Work of Dance. Labour, Movement and Identity in the 1930s*, Middletown: Wesleyan Press, 2002.

A. K. Gastev, "The Song of the Workers' Blow", in: Aleksandr Bogdanov, "Proletarian Poetry", *The Labour Monthly*, (June 1932).

Peter Gena, Jonathan Brent (Eds.), *A John Cage Reader: In Celebration of His Seventieth Birthday*, New York: C. F. Peters, 1982.

Gullermo Gomez-Peña, "In defence of Performance Art", [online], Available from: http://www.pochanostra.comantes/jazz_pocha2/mainpages/in_defense.htm (Accessed 26 January 2015).

André Gorz, *Critique of Economic Reason*, London: Verso, 1990.

Johnnie Gratton, Michael Sheringam (Eds.), *The Art of the Project*, Oxford: Berg Hahn Books, 2005.

Charles Green, *The Third Hand, Collaboration in Art from Modernism to Postmodernism*, Kensington: University of New

South Wales Press, 2001.
Boris Groys, *Gesamtkunstwerk Stalin. Die gespaltene Kultur in der Sowjiet Union*, Munich: Hanser, 1988.
Boris Groys, "Repetition of Revolution, Russian Avantgarde Revisited", [online], Available from: http://www.formerwest.org/ResearchSeminars/RussianAvantgardeRevisited/Video/RepetitionOfRevolution (Accessed 26 January 2015).
Boris Groys, "The Loneliness of the Project", *Going Public*, Berlin: Sternberg Press, 2010.
Stefano Harney, Valentina Desideri, "Fate Work: A Conversation", [online], *Ephemera*, Theory & Politics of Organization, Available from: http://www.ephemerajournal.org/contribution/fate-work-conversation (Accessed 26 January 2015).
Adrian Heathfield, *Out of Now, The Lifeworks of Tehching Hsieh*, Cambridge, Massachusetts: The MIT Press, 2009.
Daniel Heller Roazen, *Echolalias, On the Forgetting of Language*, New York: Zone Books, 2005.
Michel Houellebecq, The Map and the Territory, New York: Vintage Books, 2010.
Irwin (Ed.), *East Art Map, Contemporary Art and Eastern Europe*, London: Afterall, 2006.
Fredric Jameson, *Postmodernism, Or the Cultural Logic of Late Capitalism*, Durham, New York: Duke University Press, 1999.
Amelia Jones, *Body Art / Performing the Subject*, Minneapolis: University of Minnesota Press, 1998.
Allan Kaprow, "Notes on the creation of a Total Art", *Critical Mass: Happenings, Fluxus, Performance, Intermedia and Rutgers University*, New Brunswick: Rutgers University Press, 2003.
Peter Klepec, *Dobičkonosne strasti: Kapitalizem in perverzija*, Ljubljana: Analecta, 2008.
Eve Kosofsky Sedgwick, *Touching Feeling: Affect, Pedagogy, Performativity*, Durham, New York: Duke University Press, 2003.

Siegfried Kracauer, *The Mass Ornament*, Cambridge: Harvard University Press, 1995.
Jacques Lacan, *Television: A Challenge to the Psychoanalytic Establishment*, Edited by J. Copjec and translated by J. Mehlman, New York: W. W. Norton, 1990.
Sonja Lavaert, Pascal Gielen, "The Dismeasure of Art. An Interwiev with Paolo Virno", *Open 17: A Precarious Existence. Vulnerability in the Public Domain*, Amsterdam: SKOR (Foundation Art and Public Space), 17, (2009).
Maurizio Lazzarato, "Conversation with Maurizio Lazzaratto: Exhausting Immaterial Labour in Performance", *Le Journal des Laboratoires and TKH*, 17, (October 2010).
Maurizio Lazzarato, *The Making of the Indebted Man*, New York: Semiotext(e), 2012.
Pamela M. Lee, *Chronophobia, On Time in the Art of the 1960s*, Cambridge, London: MIT Press, 2006.
Henri Lefebvre, *The Critique of Everyday Life, Foundations for the Sociology of Everyday*, New York, London: Verso, 2002.
Henri Lefebvre, *The Production of Space*, New York: John Wiley & Sons, 1991.
Hans-Ties Lehmann, *Postdramatic Theatre*, London: Routledge, 2006.
André Lepecki, "Dance without distance", *Ballet International / Tanz Aktuell*, February 2001.
André Lepecki, *Exhausting Dance, Performance and the Politics of Movement*, New York: Routledge Champan and Hall, 2006.
Dieter Lesage, "Portrait of the Artist as a Worker", *Maska*, 5-6, 20, (2006).
Dieter Lesage, *Portrait of the Artist as a DJ, Notes on Ina Wudtke*, Brussels: VHD, 2008.
Corinne Maier, *Bonjour Paresse*, Paris: Michalon, 2004.
Boyan Manchev, "Performance time or time of performance? The struggle for duration as struggle for the event", *Maska: Projective Temporality*, 149-150, XXVII (2012).

Olivier Marchart, "In Service of the Party. A Short Genealogy of Art and Collective Activism", *Maska*, 6-7, 21, (2006).

Jean-Baptiste Marongiu, "Agamben, le chercheur d'homme", *Libération*, April 1, 1999. Also available from: http://www.liberation.fr/livres/1999/04/01/agamben-le-chercheur-d-homme_270036 (Accessed 26 January 2015).

Odo Marquard, *Temporales Doppelleben: Philosophische Bemerkugen zu unserer Zeit*, Jahburch 1990 der Deutschen Akademie für Sprache und Dichtung, Wiesbaden: Luchterland, 1990.

John Martin, *The Modern Dance*, Hightstown: Dance Horizons, 1990.

Randy Martin, *Critical Moves. Dance Studies in Theory and Politics*, Durham, New York: Duke University Press, 1998.

Karl Marx, The Capital, London: Penguin Classics, 1992.

Brian Massumi, "Navigating Movements", *Hope*, M. Zaournazzi (Ed.), New York: Routledge, 2003.

Brian Massumi, "The Future Birth of the Affective Fact", [online], *Conference Proceedings: Genealogies of Biopolitics*, Available from: http://browse.reticular.info/text/collected/massumi.pdf (Accessed 26 January 2015).

Jon McKenzie, *Perform or Else. From Discipline to Performance*, London: Routledge, 2001.

Jacques-Alain Miller, "On Shame", *Jacques Lacan and the Other side of psychoanalysis*, Justin Clemens, Russell Grigg (Eds.), Durham: Duke University Press, 2006.

Chantal Mouffe, *On The Political*, London: Routledge, 2006.

Jean-Luc Nancy, *The Inoperative Community*, Peter Connor (Ed.), Minneapolis, London: University of Minnesota Press, 2004.

Matteo Pasquinelli, "Immaterial Civil War, Prototypes of Conflict within Cognitive Capitalism", [online], Available from: http://eipcp.net/policies/cci/pasquinelli/en (Accessed 26 January 2015).

Robert Pfaller, *Das schmutzige Heilige und die reine Vernunft. Symptome der Gegenwartskultur*, Frankfurt am Main: Fischer

Verlag, 2008.

Robert Pfaller, *Wofür es sich zu leben lohnt, Elemente materialistischer Philosophie*, Frankfurt am Main: Fischer Verlag, 2011.

Yvonne Rainer, "Letter to Marina Abramović", [online], Available from: http://theperformanceclub.org/2011/11/yvonne-rainer-douglas-crimp-and-taisha-paggett-blast-marina-abramovic-and-moca-la/ (Accessed 26 January 2015).

Jacques Rancière, *Aesthetics and its Discontents*, Hoboken: John Wiley & Sons, 2009.

Jacques Rancière, *Disagreement. Politics and Philosophy*, Minneapolis: University of Minnesota Press, 1998.

Jacques Rancière, *Dissensus: On Politics and Aesthetics*, London, New York: Continuum, 2010.

Jacques Rancière, "The Emancipated Spectator", *Artforum*, (March 2007), pp. 272-280.

Jacques Rancière, *The Politics of Aesthetics, The Distribution of the Sensible*, London, New York: Continuum, 2004.

Gerald Raunig, *A Thousand Machines*, New York: Semiotext(e), 2010.

Jason Read, "The Production of Subjectivity: From Transindividuality to the Commons", *New Formations: A Journal of Culture/Theory/Politics*, 70, (July 7, 2010).

Irit Rogoff, "We - Collectivites, Mutualities, Participations", [online], Available from: http://theater.kein.org/node/95 (Accessed 26 January 2015).

Suely Rolnik, "Life on the Spot", [online], Available from: http://www.caosmose.net/suelyrolnik/index.html (Accessed 26 January, 2015).

Harmut Rosa, "Full Speed Burnout? From the Pleasures of the Motorcycle to the Bleakness of the Treadmill: The Dual Face of Social Acceleration", [online], *International Journal of Motorcycle Studies*, 6, 1, (Summer 2010), Available from: http://ijms.nova.edu/Spring2010/IJMS_Artcl.Rosa.html

(Accessed 26 January 2015).

Martha Rosler, "The Second Time as Farce", [online], *Idiom Magazine,* Available from: http://idiommag.com/2011/02/the-second-time-as-farce/ (Accessed 26 January 2015).

Renata Salecl, "Zadnje predavanje (The Last Lecture)", *Delo,* March 3, 2008.

Renata Salecl, *The Tyranny of Choice,* London: Profile Books, 2011.

Florian Schneider, "Collaboration", [online], Available from: http://summit.kein.org/node/190 (Accessed 26 January 2015).

Aaron Schuster, "Zelo težko je početi nič", [online], *Dnevnikov Objektiv,* Maša Ogrizek, (October 1, 2011), Available from: http://www.dnevnik.si/objektiv/intervjuji/1042476800 (Accessed 26 January 2015).

Richard Sennett, *The Culture of the New Capitalism,* New Haven, London: Yale University Press, 2006.

Peter Sloterdijk, "Eurotaoism, to a critique of political kinetics", *Nietzsche and the Rhetoric of Nihilism: Essays on Interpretation, Language and Politics,* Tom Darby, Béla Egyed, Ben Jones (Eds.), Ottawa: Carleton University Press, 1989.

Ivor Southwood, *Non Stop Inertia,* London: Zero Books, 2011.

Hito Steyerl, "Forget Otherness", *Another Publication,* Renee Ridgway, Katarina Zdjelar (Eds.), Berlin: Revolver, 2006.

Hito Steyerl, "Is a Museum a Factory?", *e-flux Journal,* 7, June - August 2009. Also available from: http://www.e-flux.com/journal/is-a-museum-a-factory (Accessed 26 January 2015).

Mladen Stilinović, *Artist at work: 1973–1983 = Umetnik na delu: 1973–1983,* Ljubljana: ŠKUC Gallery, 2005.

Vassilis Tsianos, Dimitris Papadopoulos, "Precarity: A Savage Journey to the Heart of Embodied Capitalism", [online], Available from: http://eipcp.net/transversal/1106/tsianospapadopoulos/en (Accessed 26 January 2015).

Myriam Van Imschoot, Xavier Le Roy, "Letters in Collaboration", *Maska,* 1-2 (84-85), 2004.

Paolo Virno, "The Dismeasure of Art", [online], Open, *A Precarious Existence*, 17 (2009), Available from: http://www.skor.nl/article-4178-en.html (Accessed 26 January 2015).

Paolo Virno, *A Grammar of the Multitude, For an Analysis of Contemporary Forms of Life*, New York: Semiote(x)te, 2004.

Marion Von Osten, "Irene ist Viele! Or What We Call 'Productive Forces'", *e-flux Journal*, (September 2009).

Max Weber, *The Protestant Ethic and the Spirit of Capitalism*, London: Routledge, 2001.

Sarah Wookey, "An Open Letter from a Dancer who refused to participate in Marina Abramovic's MOCA performance", [online], Available from: http://www.blouinartinfo.com/news/story/751666/an-open-letter-from-a-dancer-who-refused-to-participate-in-marina-abramovic%E2%80%99s-moca-performance (Accessed 26 January 2015).

Carey Young, "I'm the Revolutionary (2001)", *Incorporated*, London: Film and Video Umbrella, 2002.

Alenka Zupančič, "Lacan in sram", *Problemi, Revija za kulturo in družbena vprašanja*, 44, 7/8, (2006).

Beti Žerovc, "O umetniškem dogodku na umetniškem dogodku", Peter Kisin, Beti Žerovc (Eds.), *29. grafični bienale Ljubljana: Dogodek / The 29th Biennial of Graphic Arts: The Event*, Ljubljana: Mednarodni grafični likovni center / International Centre of Graphic Arts, 2011.

Slavoj Žižek, *Violence: Six Sideways Reflections*, London: Profile Books, 2009.

Videos

Marina Abramović, Sanford Kwinter, *A Conversation*, [online], video. Available from: http://youtu.be/iIL7stvnvBs (Accessed 26 January 2015).

Chris Burden, *Documentation of Selected Works 1971–1975*, [online], film, 35 min. Available from: http://www.ubu.com/film/burden.html (Accessed 26 January 2015).

Chto Delat?, *The Builders*, [online], video, 8 min. Available from: http://vimeo.com/6878627 (Accessed 26 January 2015).

Harun Farocki, *Arbeiter Verlassen die Fabrik (Workers leaving the factory)*, [online], video, 36 min, 1995. Available from: https://vimeo.com/59338090 (Accessed 26 January 2015).

Dr. Seuss: *Pontoffel Pock, Where Are You*, DVD, 25 min, Universal Studios, 2003.

Igor Štromajer, Brane Zorman, *Ballettikka Internettikka: Stattikka*, video, 6 min, 2007. Available from: http://www.intima.org/bi/stattikka (Accessed 26 January 2015).

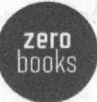

Contemporary culture has eliminated both the concept of the public and the figure of the intellectual. Former public spaces – both physical and cultural – are now either derelict or colonized by advertising. A cretinous anti-intellectualism presides, cheerled by expensively educated hacks in the pay of multinational corporations who reassure their bored readers that there is no need to rouse themselves from their interpassive stupor. The informal censorship internalized and propagated by the cultural workers of late capitalism generates a banal conformity that the propaganda chiefs of Stalinism could only ever have dreamt of imposing. Zer0 Books knows that another kind of discourse – intellectual without being academic, popular without being populist – is not only possible: it is already flourishing, in the regions beyond the striplit malls of so-called mass media and the neurotically bureaucratic halls of the academy. Zer0 is committed to the idea of publishing as a making public of the intellectual. It is convinced that in the unthinking, blandly consensual culture in which we live, critical and engaged theoretical reflection is more important than ever before.

ZERO BOOKS

If this book has helped you to clarify an idea, solve a problem or extend your knowledge, you may like to read more titles from Zero Books. Recent bestsellers are:

Capitalist Realism Is there no alternative?
Mark Fisher
An analysis of the ways in which capitalism has presented itself as the only realistic political-economic system.
Paperback: November 27, 2009 978-1-84694-317-1 $14.95 £7.99.
eBook: July 1, 2012 978-1-78099-734-6 $9.99 £6.99.

The Wandering Who? A study of Jewish identity politics
Gilad Atzmon
An explosive unique crucial book tackling the issues of Jewish Identity Politics and ideology and their global influence.
Paperback: September 30, 2011 978-1-84694-875-6 $14.95 £8.99.
eBook: September 30, 2011 978-1-84694-876-3 $9.99 £6.99.

Clampdown Pop-cultural wars on class and gender
Rhian E. Jones
Class and gender in Britpop and after, and why 'chav' is a feminist issue.
Paperback: March 29, 2013 978-1-78099-708-7 $14.95 £9.99.
eBook: March 29, 2013 978-1-78099-707-0 $7.99 £4.99.

The Quadruple Object
Graham Harman
Uses a pack of playing cards to present Harman's metaphysical system of fourfold objects, including human access, Heidegger's indirect causation, panpsychism and ontography.
Paperback: July 29, 2011 978-1-84694-700-1 $16.95 £9.99.

Weird Realism Lovecraft and Philosophy
Graham Harman
As Hölderlin was to Martin Heidegger and Mallarmé to Jacques Derrida, so is H.P. Lovecraft to the Speculative Realist philosophers.
Paperback: September 28, 2012 978-1-78099-252-5 $24.95 £14.99.
eBook: September 28, 2012 978-1-78099-907-4 $9.99 £6.99.

Sweetening the Pill or How We Got Hooked on Hormonal Birth Control
Holly Grigg-Spall
Is it really true? Has contraception liberated or oppressed women?
Paperback: September 27, 2013 978-1-78099-607-3 $22.95 £12.99.
eBook: September 27, 2013 978-1-78099-608-0 $9.99 £6.99.

Why Are We The Good Guys? Reclaiming Your Mind From The Delusions Of Propaganda
David Cromwell
A provocative challenge to the standard ideology that Western power is a benevolent force in the world.
Paperback: September 28, 2012 978-1-78099-365-2 $26.95 £15.99.
eBook: September 28, 2012 978-1-78099-366-9 $9.99 £6.99.

The Truth about Art Reclaiming quality
Patrick Doorly
The book traces the multiple meanings of art to their various sources, and equips the reader to choose between them.
Paperback: August 30, 2013 978-1-78099-841-1 $32.95 £19.99.

Bells and Whistles More Speculative Realism
Graham Harman
In this diverse collection of sixteen essays, lectures, and interviews Graham Harman lucidly explains the principles of

Speculative Realism, including his own object-oriented philosophy.
Paperback: November 29, 2013 978-1-78279-038-9 $26.95 £15.99.
eBook: November 29, 2013 978-1-78279-037-2 $9.99 £6.99.

Towards Speculative Realism: Essays and Lectures Essays and Lectures
Graham Harman
These writings chart Harman's rise from Chicago sportswriter to co founder of one of Europe's most promising philosophical movements: Speculative Realism.
Paperback: November 26, 2010 978-1-84694-394-2 $16.95 £9.99.
eBook: January 1, 1970 978-1-84694-603-5 $9.99 £6.99.

Meat Market Female flesh under capitalism
Laurie Penny
A feminist dissection of women's bodies as the fleshy fulcrum of capitalist cannibalism, whereby women are both consumers and consumed.
Paperback: April 29, 2011 978-1-84694-521-2 $12.95 £6.99.
eBook: May 21, 2012 978-1-84694-782-7 $9.99 £6.99.

Translating Anarchy The Anarchism of Occupy Wall Street
Mark Bray
An insider's account of the anarchists who ignited Occupy Wall Street.
Paperback: September 27, 2013 978-1-78279-126-3 $26.95 £15.99.
eBook: September 27, 2013 978-1-78279-125-6 $6.99 £4.99.

One Dimensional Woman
Nina Power
Exposes the dark heart of contemporary cultural life by examining pornography, consumer capitalism and the ideology of women's work.

Paperback: November 27, 2009 978-1-84694-241-9 $14.95 £7.99.
eBook: July 1, 2012 978-1-78099-737-7 $9.99 £6.99.

Dead Man Working
Carl Cederstrom, Peter Fleming
An analysis of the dead man working and the way in which capital is now colonizing life itself.
Paperback: May 25, 2012 978-1-78099-156-6 $14.95 £9.99.
eBook: June 27, 2012 978-1-78099-157-3 $9.99 £6.99.

Unpatriotic History of the Second World War
James Heartfield
The Second World War was not the Good War of legend. James Heartfield explains that both Allies and Axis powers fought for the same goals - territory, markets and natural resources.
Paperback: September 28, 2012 978-1-78099-378-2 $42.95 £23.99.
eBook: September 28, 2012 978-1-78099-379-9 $9.99 £6.99.

Find more titles at www.zero-books.net

www.ingramcontent.com/pod-product-compliance
Lightning Source LLC
Chambersburg PA
CBHW011404210526
45464CB00010B/3039